MW01141914

Note for Librarians: A cataloguing record for this book is available from Library and Archives
Canada at www.collectionscanada.ca/amicus/index-e.html
ISBN 1-4120-8064-9

PUBLISHING

Offices in Canada, USA, Ireland and UK
This book was published *on-demand* in cooperation with Trafford Publishing. On-demand
publishing is a unique process and service of making a book available for retail sale to the
public taking advantage of on-demand manufacturing and Internet marketing. On-demand
publishing includes promotions, retail sales, manufacturing, order fulfilment, accounting and
collecting royalties on behalf of the author.

Book sales for North America and international:
Trafford Publishing, 6E–2333 Government St.,
Victoria, BC V8T 4P4 CANADA
phone 250 383 6864 (toll-free 1 888 232 4444)
fax 250 383 6804; email to orders@trafford.com
Book sales in Europe:
Trafford Publishing (UK) Limited, 9 Park End Street, 2nd Floor
Oxford, UK OX1 1HH UNITED KINGDOM
phone 44 (0)1865 722 113 (local rate 0845 230 9601)
facsimile 44 (0)1865 722 868; info.uk@trafford.com
Order online at:
trafford.com/05-3062
10 9 8 7 6 5 4 3

To my husband, my everything, your support and encouragement kept me going no matter what.

To my daughter Amanda and sons Brock and LJ, thank you for allowing me to share so many can grow. It is my prayer that you continue to use the tools in this book to achieve your hearts wildest desires. I am so proud to call you my children.

To all the characters whose influence evoked a reference in this work. You won't recognize your name because I changed it and I apologize if my recollections do not match yours but I thank you for your impact on my life.

To my sweet niece Autumn, you were right; we are decedents of Rudolf Horst and we not only can, we did do it. Thank you for holding my hand through this process. I could not have done it without you, your talents, your support and your love. I thank you from the bottom of my heart.

Table of Contents

My Turn

Introduction

I've heard it said that God speaks in the places you are listening. Of course, we all have different ways of hearing Him and mine has always been through writings. At first it wasn't in my writing where I heard God's voice. It was in other writings; that of educators, promoters, even everyday anonymous news rag astrologers. It wasn't so much about what was written there on the page, it was more about how it hit me in the heart—any time I was looking for hope, an answer, wisdom, God found a way to get it to me in every place I was looking, at every stage of my understanding. God will speak in any place as long as we are willing to listen. And only when we are ready, will the message be received as truth.

1

I stood behind the curtain in the dark, listening for my cue to go on stage. The brush of the heavy velvet on my hand reminded me of the many times I had passed through this way, as a dancer, or as a teacher, and the many times since, as Miss Noelle, the owner and artistic director of Jellison Studios; but this time was different because it would be the last time. I would not return to the stage again. The crowd cheers for the final dance and the girls skip by giving me high fives and quick hugs on their way to the backstage.

The M.C. comes to the microphone and begins to say goodbye. He is saying goodbye to me.

"Miss Noelle has been an asset to our community; she has inspired dance and artistic expression in hundreds upon hundreds of children in this town. Her instruction has given dreams to those who dance for recreation, and wings to the many of our children who have gone on to dance on the international stage. Noelle has led our children to dance for Royalty, at the World Expo and on CBC television specials. As individuals, under Noelle, many of our children have won accolades in competition and acceptance in major cities and honorable productions. They have danced in the Orient, Europe, and on virtually every stage worth naming in North America, including the Royal Winnipeg Ballet and the National Ballet of Canada.

Noelle has been a cheerleader, mentor, confidant, and even at times, a surrogate mother for each one of her little dancers.

On behalf of the City of Fort St. John and our Arts Council, we thank you Noelle for your tireless contribution to the lives of the people in this community, for bringing out our talents and sharing so much of yourself with us. We thank you!"

The crowd came to their feet as I passed onto the stage to accept the last bouquet of roses that I would ever accept for my role in dance.

The M.C.'s words, and my view of an applauding audience, filled my heart with feelings of regret, sadness, anticipation for a normal life and gratitude that I had had the opportunity to work and live in this little Northern city. My head swam in the moment as my dancers swarmed onto the stage to kiss and say goodbye, and as I left the stage, I felt it—I was walking into a new life. Walking away from a life that had held me captive from the time I was twenty years old . . . the day I met Elward.

2

He was a dream. The classic tall, dark, and handsome, poetic, pensive, strong, silent, romantic type, and better still, he was quickly head over heels in love with me. I was a dancer, preparing to be a dance instructor—it was what I always knew I would be—and he was on his way to school to get his business management degree. We were a match made of all the right stuff and we knew that together, life would be bliss.

~

Three children, a dance studio, and an education later, Elward and I had arrived. We had it all. We worked hard during the school months. I did everything, and Elward did everything I didn't get to. Between the two of us, we covered the work of six people. The first three hours of my day were spent cleaning an office building, coaching my kids through private dance practice, and then getting everyone back home for breakfast and dressed for school—all before eight-thirty in the morning. I couldn't keep that up for more than a few years, so when the kids were old enough to help, we put off the cleaning until the evening and reserved the mornings for their dance instead. I did my best at keeping up with my motherly duties; dishes, laundry, dropping off lunches to schools, going to work on hot dog day, attending the school assemblies—all before noon. After lunch I went to my studio building and managed our little retail store which carried dance supplies, and when there were no customers, I organized my teaching day. I tried to stay on top of the day to day business which always seemed like a lost cause. At nine o'clock in the evening when I was done teaching, we would head off as a family to do the cleaning of two office buildings.

On Saturdays I taught private lessons and small groups at the studio usually from seven-thirty in the morning to six o'clock at night and from January to the end of competition season I taught Sundays as well. Fridays were my only true day off. But when summer came and the studio grew quiet, we took every opportunity to build exotic and fun-filled memories for our children. Every weekend became a long weekend, taking off on Friday and coming back late Sunday to clean the buildings.

Our kids would only be kids for a few years and we didn't want to miss a minute of it. No matter what they were doing, Elward and I were in it with them; supporting, laughing, helping and loving them. We lived for the trips— getting away from the everyday, hitting the beaches of Cape Canaveral, and the dance competitions in Orlando, Las Vegas, and Los Angeles. If I had to do it all over again I wouldn't change a thing. Those memories of our family are forever printed on our hearts. I can remember being on our last dollar—credit cards maxed out—but we still found a way to squeeze in our weekly weekend getaway.

When I think back now, it is like a dream—our summer trips were an oasis on the desert of a very busy, very stressful work life. Even now, so many years later, the memories of the vacation times take me to a place of total serenity. I can smell the salt water, taste the wind, hear the call of the gulls as the boys cheer and hop on the deck of our white twenty-six foot power sailboat. Elward makes the call and the boat soars out into the bay. The water is silent, smooth. The anchor is down, and now Elward is pulling up the trap. There will be thick crab legs dipped in hot butter tonight served with fresh salmon steaks, baby potatoes and crisp green beans. There will be laughter and stories and dreams about good times to come. As the quiet comes over us, Amanda will sit on the hull, her long, dark hair will flit from her shoulders and back, and the sun will set over her head, a golden halo, kissing her slight shoulders as the night draws on. Then later, when three children are asleep, with moonbeams skipping across the surface of the water and the lightning of phosphorescence replying from below, Elward will wrap his arms around me and call me Mrs. J. and the waves will rock us and everything in the world will be right.

Dear Reader, we had it all. I swear, we had it all! It was there, in those moments—the peace, the love, the incredible joy. I held it all in the palm of my hand, but it was not mine to grasp, not mine to keep.

In our home town, we were a raving success story. Our kids; LJ, Brock, and Amanda were great dancers. They excelled in everything they did and we were so proud. I didn't have to push really, they were the kind of kids who had ambition and who really wanted to please their parents. LJ, our young Elward look-alike could woo a crowd like no other. He was great looking, athletic and determined. He chose modern Jazz as his way of expression and was a star in every way. When he moved, the audience couldn't look away. They couldn't help but be drawn in. When LJ danced, it was magic.

Brock, our sandy-blonde son was bright and funny. He chose tap dance as his specialty and he was incredible. He could keep an audience on the edge of their seats with just the tap of his toe and the intensity that radiated from every part of him. He loved musical theatre and no matter what he did, it was like theatre—intense and wild and oh, so funny. His success as an entertainer was as sure as the dawn and as bright as that sun. When Brock danced it was pure energy.

Amanda. My Amanda. So beautiful and disciplined and graceful. She was a perfectionist by nature and she put everything she had into dancing. She pushed herself, beyond pain, and beyond her years to become exceptional in all mediums of dance from ballet to contemporary. I wanted the world for her. Elward and I would be certain to give it to her. Oh, how I loved what my little girl was becoming. Everything. I loved everything about her, and when Amanda danced it was pure inspiration.

The small Northern community could not hold my kids forever. They had ambition that exceeded what I could give them, and talent that burst the boundaries of our community. LJ was the first to say he needed more.

"Mom, for one minute, I need you to think with your head and not your heart." It was the one line knock-out blow in a battle that I could never win. The one thing he could say to convince me that he was ready to move out of our home. LJ was only a kid, but he knew what he wanted and he knew that in the end, it was what I wanted for him too. I had trained my children, driven them to be great. Now LJ, desperate to go in search of his dream, had found a reasonable way out. He wanted to go live with another instructor, a dear friend of mine who lived in Calgary, a major center where LJ could study and truly excel. I guess I always knew it would happen, but it never dawned on me that he might leave at such a young age. He was just sixteen. I was torn.

Losing LJ would mean a huge change for the whole family and my heart would have to stretch from Northern BC to Southern Alberta to reach him and keep him safe. I trusted Susan though, and so, it was decided. We would miss him, but we knew that Susan would fill in whatever void was left as we parted ways. We let LJ go. And his dreams began coming true when we did.

Brock, just a year younger than LJ, worked hard to study dance and to graduate from high school. Upon graduation he was quickly picked up by a professional group called *Tap Dogs*—*"The Hottest Show on Legs"*— and he was amazing! My young comedian wowed the crowd in every show he danced.

By the time Brock left, LJ was dancing for Disney in Japan. We were happy for Brock and thrilled for LJ, and we were worried sick about Amanda.

3

One day, Amanda and I were on a cleaning frenzy. Everything in our home needed to be taken apart, washed out and set straight. It was the first week of August and we had guest teachers coming to stay with us to do two weeks of intensive workshops at the studio. Major clean-ups like this one only happened twice a year—once for the summer teachers and once at Christmas.

The day started out fine, but the mess always bothered Amanda and the time crunch set us both on our last nerve. When we exploded it was a long drawn out explosion, and looking back now I can understand why. Just like our busy cluttered house, Amanda and I had busy, cluttered, stressed-out selves, so when the clean up began, we cleaned up our souls with it and let out every frustration in a terrible, brutal, verbal cleansing that shook the house and brought Elward in from the garage.

"That's enough!" Amanda and I stopped cold. Elward never ever raised his voice. Never!

"I've had enough of this. I cannot and will not take this anymore!"

He took Amanda outside to work with him and left me to finish in the house by myself. He wasn't angry, but he was so frustrated. This was happening way too often and he could see a loving mother and daughter relationship disintegrating very quickly.

I spent the day in the house crying. The sting of Amanda's words and the fire of my own—so sad, so disgusting.

Elward and I didn't talk about it until later, when we climbed into bed.

"I'm sorry Elward. I am so sorry. I really lost it with her today. I didn't mean it. I didn't mean to react so badly. I just don't know why she snaps the way she does."

"I don't know Noelle. Are you pushing her buttons?"

"Maybe it's just that I'm pushing her. I love her, I want what is best for her. . .I want her to be happy—not just now—but later, when she looks back on her life."

"Is it too much?" He asked.

"I think it's what she wants. She wants to be great. She pushes herself just as hard as I push her."

"Did I tell you about Dr. Brar?" Elward flipped on his side to face me.

"No."

"His wife saw Amanda snap on you the other night at the theatre and he. . ."

"Oh, no! Elward, I . . ." *I am so embarrassed.*

"—he talked to me at the clinic the other night and suggested he could see Amanda and get her on a low dose of meds to take the edge off the mood swings, y'know to help with the stress."

"Drugs?! Oh, for heaven's sake Elward, she's not crazy!"

"Well, that's just what I told him. I *know* she's not crazy, but we need to do something."

There was a long silence as we both thought about what 'something' could be. Elward wrapped his arms around me and started to drift. I heard his breath, felt the heave of his chest against my back. His arm got heavier and my heart did too. I lay there, for a long time, the clock ticking like a hammer on pavement. Sleep would not come, but something else did. Suddenly, I knew. I saw clearly my relationship with Amanda and it made me sick.

"Elward?"

"Mmmhmmm?"

"I can't stop thinking."

"What about?"

"Amanda, and me. Oh, no. How did I miss this? How could I not see my own daughter suffering, when she was suffering so badly?" I started to shake and moved out from under his arm.

"Are you okay?"

"No. I'm not. I mean listen. I've always been her dance teacher and not so much her mother. I mean, you know we have a good relationship, but the other kids have me to instruct and their mothers to dote and encourage. It's like I have only been able to give to her what I was willing to give to two hundred and fifty other kids and that's not good enough. It was never good enough." The shakes have turned to tears. *I thought I had cried all of my tears today.*

"Noelle, don't be so hard on your self. You have been an amazing mother to all of our. . ."

"No. Stop. Let me finish this." He rolled back on his shoulders and let me go on.

"Amanda is always last. The last for costumes, choreography, counseling. When there are three girls crying, she's the last I console. When there is hair, and rollers and makeup, she's the last in line. Last, last, last. Dammit Elward, she should be first. She should have always been first and I have spent so much time trying not to play favorites at the studio, for fear of what the moms might have thought of me. I forgot that Amanda is the only girl that counts here and I have let her down. She should be first Elward. I need to make her first for once—or we are going to lose her and she'll be gone and she's only fifteen Elward." Then it hit me. "Elward, she's *already* fifteen and I haven't let her know that she comes first." I was wracked with sobs and heaves of pain and regret and desperation and when I was done I turned to see Elward, his hands near his face and a single tear rolling on his cheek.

The next day it was decided. Drugs would never be the answer for stress, and Amanda was, no doubt, under great stress. We would work to change her world and we would call on my brother Tony to heal her body.

Tony had had his own set of problems with health in his family, in fact, his wife had killed herself and a few of his kids were being treated for various mood disorders. He and his friend David had developed a nutritional supplement for the kids and had managed to get a group of researchers to study the effects of the supplement at a local university. They discovered that it not only helped with mood disorders, but it helped many other stress related physical ailments. It was just what she needed.

Tony sent us the bottles and Amanda took the supplements religiously. She started to improve immediately. While Amanda got stronger and calmer, we worked on a long-term plan to change what was left of our parenting years.

We decided to leave the North and get to a metropolis where she would be able to further develop her career in dance and modeling. We would move to Vancouver.

4

Our decision to move was huge for me. Huge! Realizing I truly wanted to drop everything and move for Amanda—to save her life—made me assess my own. Like snapping to after a twenty-year coma, I woke up—exhausted. My dancer body was gone and I was carrying one hundred extra pounds of fat on my mid-section. My two sons were off traveling the world, dancing and building careers for themselves, Amanda was sick with stress, and our finances, like a boil set deep under the skin, suddenly came to a hot blistering reality. Elward got laid off from his job as an oilfield dispatcher. Now, with more than half of our income gone and no chance of employment for Elward in this town we had to speed up our plans to move. We were just over four hundred thousand dollars in debt and our dream boat was sinking fast. How did it come to this when everything seemed so great for so long? How?

We had to sell the house in order to move, but like my body, it had been neglected through many years of coming and going and rushing around, and in a brutally competitive market, it would need a full renovation. We went to the bank for the money for the renovation and when that ran out borrowed from Elward's father. Now, including the dance studio and odd loans over the years, we were indebted to him for over three hundred thousand dollars of our debt. We were banking on a good sale price for the house—it would help with some of the debt and get us into a place in Vancouver. Then it happened. More and more lay offs happened. The main industry in town slumped and our worst nightmare came true. The bottom fell out of the housing market. Everyone was running to sell and get out of town to find work. Realizing that liquidating our assets, (the house and the dance building), in a broken market would not pay the amount owing on the properties, we went into survival mode.

And it was up to Elward to explain that need for survival to his father.

"Dad, even if we manage to sell the house, we'll be taking a major hit. The market is so bad right now and we are going to need something to go on, to get set up in Vancouver." Elward hates saying these words.

"What are you saying?" Dad acts naive.

"I'm saying, even if we sell the place, we won't be able to pay off the debt right away." We all shift in our kitchen chairs as the words fall from Elward's lips to the floor.

"The house is collateral on the loan. You can't sell it and leave me holding an unsecured loan." Dad leans into Elward and I get right out of my chair.

The stress, my desperation makes me insolent.

"You are worried about the flipping loan? What's the matter with you? We are family and we are trying to do what is best for your grand-daughter. She's *your* grand-daughter. You are just going to have to wait. It's not our fault that the market sucks. It's not our fault!"

I am shaking and yelling and Elward can't stop me—but his father will try. He hollers back and I respond and the situation escalates, and Elward puts his head in his hands.

~

We left town and the house did not sell, but it was better that way because at least the rental income from the dance building and the house would cover our minimum payments to Dad and the bank. We'd just have to come up with the moving money from some other place.

Homeless and jobless, we entered a race fueled on scrounged money. We took a second mortgage on the house to fund the move and borrowed money against the borrowed money—buying time and covering bills and getting us into a rental near Vancouver. Now, we desperately needed work—before the next round of bills came in. We hadn't seen it before, when the money was rolling in from all of our jobs, but with the debt load we were carrying we couldn't go a month, not two weeks, not even two days without income.

It didn't take long for me to discover that there wasn't a lot of gainful employment in the big city for a former dance teacher and an overqualified oil field dispatcher. Now, Dear Reader, the madness begins.

5

Until now, we had been lucky. Elward's father had served as a bank for us, lending huge chunks of his estate to help us along the way. But after our falling out over the loans and our inability to liquidate our assets, he was left holding the bag and his generosity was no longer a benefit to us or an asset to him. Every day, Elward suffered. Like a bullhorn in the ear—his father's silence screamed through Elward's whole being. And when the silence was broken, it was worse than the screaming bullhorn . . .

~

It was another warm and cloudy day; I stepped outside in my bare feet to reach into the mailbox. A few bills reared their ugly heads, and then, fumbling past the bills, I found a letter, addressed by hand. It was not a bill. My heart flipped with hope. This was probably a welcome exchange from LJ or Brock, or a letter from my mother. I love hand written mail—little thank-you notes or postcards are a gift to the receiver. It means something to make that effort and when someone does it for you, you know they care.

I dropped the bills on the coffee table and opened the note.

"Dear Elward and Noelle,

I have thought and rethought, hashed and rehashed the events of our meeting . . ."

Before I got past the first paragraph, I dropped to the couch, thanking God that Elward was not here to read this himself . . . that he would never, ever read it. I'd be sure of that.

Elward didn't need to read this—the venom and the accusation, the incredible misunderstanding heaped upon insult, vile cruelty, and name calling. He didn't understand why we had moved, why we couldn't pay out the debt, and he could never understand as long as he was so very bitter. I sent a letter back and attempted to explain to him that we were doing our best and that I refused to show his son the letter. Admittedly, I flung a little mud in his direction because my heart was so hurt—I didn't care if I ever spoke to him again. What hurt more though was that I had been party to smashing a relationship between a father and a son. He was, after all, my husband's father and someday they would need each other.

I didn't tell Elward about the letter or my reply for awhile. When I finally told him, it was a brief explanation that his Dad was angry about our debt and our inability to repay what we owed. I told him that his Dad blamed me for the financial problems and Elward knew that wasn't wholly true. So, Elward, being the loyal, loving husband that he has always been, stood with me and defended me with *his* silence.

Every morning, Elward got up and went off to his work. Outdoor work, constructing and hauling, hammering and shoveling, slamming massive slabs of concrete around, watching the results of his labor as the buildings took shape. He loved the work. He came in every day with a deeper tan and a stronger mind. It was so good for him. Hard work can heal a lot of things, resolve a lot of sadness and mental fatigue, but it cannot heal a broken heart.

There is just something about a boy and his Dad. They need each other, and Elward grieved for his father. It was bad enough, humiliating enough, to be so indebted to him, but when he felt like the debt had destroyed the relationship it was like a death in the family. The pain for him was paralyzing, but I didn't see it until I found him on the couch one morning.

He lay like he was dead. Nothing moved on him, but his eyes were still open. I walked right up to him.

"Elward. Elward! Hon are you okay?" He didn't move. I sat on the floor next to his head and touched his hair, afraid to touch the skin, in case it was cold. He was so still. Then, the tears began to flow. He never moved, only the tears rolled and streaked over his face, disappearing into his dark mustache, and pooling in his lips. He was so very still.

"Hon, you are scaring me." I let the words out, but knew as I said it that this wasn't about me, so I held him the way he would have held me and let him go on saying nothing.

Nothing. It was all he could do, and all I could do to change it. *Nothing*.

6

Nothing? Okay, well, there was something I could do to help. I decided since I was not finding any decent work, I'd have to take whatever I could find. There were no dance studios or appropriate workplaces with openings in the area, so I decided it might be fun to go back to work as a waitress. I had done really well as a waitress when I was in school. Really well. I made so many tips I could live off of them alone and save the income—or in this case, apply it to our debt. I was the kind of waitress that took care of people. The ultimate multi-tasker with a memory like no other. My customers loved me. I made them laugh and they always came back.

I dropped my resume off at a few great restaurants in the neighborhood. Waiting tables again would be great. I even found one place that had a 'Help Wanted' sign in the window. The assistant manager accepted my resume on the spot and told me to come back the next day for an interview.

I woke up the next morning feeling hopeful. I dressed up smart and got there with time to spare.

"Hi, breakfast for one?" The petit brunette in the black miniskirt offers me a seat.

"Hi, ... oh, no. I'm here to see Kenny."

"Can I tell him who is waiting?"

"I'm Noelle, I just dropped my resume by yesterday—the assistant manager told me to come by for an interview at ten this morning." I smiled, she seemed sweet.

"Oh. Really?" She took a step back and looked me over from head to toe and back up—resting on my torso for about three seconds too long. "Have a seat. I'll go tell him you are here." *Okay, maybe not so sweet.*

She went into the back and I heard voices. I waited a few minutes before she appeared again. "Yeah, sorry about that, Kenny isn't able to interview right now."

"Oh, well I'm a little early. I was told ten. Um, should I wait?"

"You can if you want to." She spun on her heel and skipped back to work.

I sat in the entry way watching diners come and go, the brunch crowd left and the lunch crowd started to trickle in. *He's not coming out Noelle.*

I waited and waited and the longer I waited the angrier I became.

The brunette went on a break and when I was still there when she came back, she was clearly annoyed.

"Kenny isn't giving an interview today ma'am."

"I'd like to talk to him."

"I already asked."

"I want to talk to him." I know if I can just talk to him he'll see past my weight.

She didn't know how to get rid of me, so she stepped back into the kitchen. Again the voices, again the long wait. And laughter. I heard laughter. When she came back, she couldn't get the smirk off her face.

"Kenny says he's not here. It's probably best if you go look somewhere else for a job." It stung so badly. I had never felt that before, the stinging stigma of obesity.

In a town where I was respected, my talents revered, my weight just seemed a part of me. People knew how hard I worked. People just accepted that Noelle, the Artistic Director, Hospital Board Director, member of the local arts council, and mother of three was who she was and looked how she looked and I held my head up and never once considered that my weight was a liability. Now, in a new place where people did not know who I was, it was a terrible liability. My body did not inspire confidence in my ability to teach dance or even to wait tables. People in my old life respected me for what I did and who I was. People in my new life saw only a very fat middle-aged woman without a job. For the first time in my life I hung my head and left empty handed. The same scenario played out day after day until there was nothing left of my pride. At two hundred and sixty pounds I was simply unemployable. But I needed a job so badly. I begged and cried and prayed for help. *Oh, God, please help.*

Then, relief. I walked into a Subway sandwich store and talked to a young kid, maybe nineteen. He was the day manager of the shop and the owner rarely came in. He and I hit it off. I made him laugh. He hired me on the spot and I started training the next day. Subway. It wasn't what I wanted. But it was something I could do to try to make things better. Somehow, we'd pay back Elward's dad and heal this broken mess of a relationship.

It didn't matter that I'd be working at Subway. No one would know. I'd do this job until I found better work, until we got back on our feet.

7

I worked the day shift at Subway. Lots of anonymity here. The only people coming in were kids from the high school and a few local workers or passer-bys. This is not a job I could have done back home in my old life. I could never have let people see me in this uniform and behind this countertop. And thankfully, they never would. *Hmmm, never say never.*

"Hi, I'd like cold cut combo on wheat. Please." A man blusters in from the street. He sounds hungry.

"Would you like Swiss or cheddar?"

"Cheddar—Hey, um, aren't you the woman that use to teach my kids dance?"

"I don't know, am I?" I didn't recognize this balding blonde man.

"Oh, yeah, up North." He was sure now. Dammit. "So that's what you did with all that money. You bought a franchise? Good on ya!"

I couldn't find my words before the sandwich artist next to me piped up with a hearty laugh,

"Ha! Oh, she doesn't own the place, she just *works* here."

The man was obviously embarrassed for me. He took a step back and I finished his order with very few words and no eye contact. I didn't remember him; he was one of hundreds and hundreds of parents over too many years. He was one face in a packed theatre—I would get over the exposure quickly and he was sure to forget. *Right?*

The day came when I was to be trained enough to open all by myself. I had so much to remember—so many things to do. Put out the bread and turn on the proofing oven. *Or was it, turn on the oven and put out the bread?* Start the coffee; fill all the front trays with the meats, veggies and condiments. *A colorful pallet for true artists!* Then, fill the cash register, make the first batch of bread and deli buns plus take care of anyone who came in for breakfast. I was really struggling. Multitasking has always come easily to me when it mattered, but now I could not remember a thing that they had told me to do. A very unimpressed store owner sat on a stool by the ovens watching me fumble and fluster.

By the time I got to work the debit machine, he'd had it with me. He didn't say much, he just huffed a garlic breath and stepped into my space—forcing me to the side and taking over at the register.

Later that day, the kid that hired me told me I was not ready to be opening the store. What a hit on my self-confidence. *Hello, we're talking Subway here.* What a blow to the ego.

I didn't want to excel in Subway service. I didn't want to be a Sandwich Artist. I just wanted to go home.

The day after I failed the morning opener routine I had to drag myself into the store. I came in the back way and tried to perk myself up in the staff room with a happy glance in the mirror. I can do this. I can do it for Elward and I can do it for Amanda. *Okay, really, I can do this. It's only a six hour shift.*

The store owner pokes his scrawny head out of the back office as I try to slip past to the storefront. Oh, no. He's the last person I need to see today.

"What are you wearing?"

"My uniform." I speak and walk.

"No, Stop." I stop. "That's not the uniform. The uniform requires black pants. Those are not black. They are charcoal at best."

I look down and lift my leg to see my pants past my belly. They are the same pants he saw me in yesterday. I can't turn to talk to him; he'll see it in my face, the anger, the desperation—and not all for him, not because he had to pick at me today. He'll see I am angry at myself for being here at all, I want to tell him I am better than this job, that I don't belong here, that I have managed staff and orchestrated dancers—that just five years ago, I could have bought the store from under him.

"They are the darkest pants I own."

"Get darker ones."

"I can't afford. . ."

"Get darker ones."

I risk his anger as I walk away. But if I don't leave now, I'll surely be leaving out the back door and jobless.

The morning is slow, cold cuts and fresh bread melt into mayonnaise and Italian dressing and salt and pepper shakes—one after the other until I hear the noon bell of the high school ring. Will she come today? Oh, I pray she will come today. And in an instant, she is in the window, through the doorway. Amanda. She is laughing and sharing a high school secret. She stops to wave hello as she steps into line. I pause, remember why I am here, and that it is worth it to see her now. Her smooth chestnut hair bouncing off her slight shoulders, her fresh face, graceful happiness in a crowd of friends. They are moving in a pack the way young girls do, all with clear skin, straight teeth, giggles and flirts; healthy girls, with my healthy daughter.

"I'll have a veggie lover's on brown." The man in front of me brings me back and I am happy to make this sandwich. Today, every sandwich is for Amanda.

8

Not long after I started working, I got a phone call from my dear friend Sylvia. She told me she had been transferred from Fort St. John to Vancouver. It was so great to hear from someone who knew the real me.

"Really? Sylvia, that's fantastic! When did you transfer to Vancouver?"

"Oh, just last month. I have been going crazy getting settled, and I couldn't wait to connect with you again. Wanna do lunch? I know a great place on Robson."

"Friday?"

"Always!"

It was settled. We would meet on Friday and I was thrilled. For one afternoon, I would re-enter my old life. The life when doing lunch was a favorite Friday pastime, and friends like Sylvia were mine. I had kept a calendar to keep my Fridays straight. And my social calendar was always full.

I loved, loved, loved Fridays back home in my other life. We didn't have to clean on Fridays, and I closed the studio early. Friday afternoons were good times with my friends and Friday nights belonged to Elward. As soon as the kids were settled, we'd sneak off to the bedroom with Boston Pizza appetizers, Hagen Dazs ice cream—two spoons, sometimes a movie, but always a plan for a night of love and laughter. The memories of Friday nights and Saturday mornings carried me through the week—and I could make it through anything as long as I knew Friday was coming soon. My Friday with Sylvia couldn't come soon enough. So when the day finally crept up on the calendar, I was ready.

I made sure I looked great that day; I would not go for lunch looking like a woman who was busy battling back the demons in her closet. I was embarrassed of those demonic haunts, the demon of debt, the demon of self-doubt and self- pity. . .and worst of all this Friday, the demon of Sandwich Artist employment. Sylvia must never know that these demons had become my constant companions. I would put on a confident radiance for Sylvia and we would have a lovely lunch together.

I arrived just in time to meet her outside her office building. She worked in one of the towers, the kind with a view. The kind filled with happy people, satisfied with their lives, their careers and their fabulous fashion forward clothing. Sylvia breezed through the front glass entry like a runway model draped in wool and silk as soft as her sleek black hair.

"Sylvia, I can't believe it! So good to see you."

"And you. Noelle, you look great. Oh, I've missed you. So nice to see a familiar face." She stoops a little. We hug and kiss cheeks and it feels like a true Friday to me already.

"It's raining," says Sylvia, "d'you mind walking?"

"Heck no! What's Vancouver without rain?"

Sylvia pops up her deep blue umbrella. And I step under with her. I can't help but admire her perfectly tailored suit jacket and the way it skims her hips. I give my jacket a tug to keep it from riding up and fall in step with her. We are so different, but Sylvia doesn't seem to notice or care. Our conversation never misses a beat and it is just like old times again.

Just a few blocks and we arrive at a fabulous Oriental food restaurant.

We sit down to steamed rice, and a table of authentic cuisine. Barbequed duck, diced chicken, shrimp and cashews in a bird's nest of crispy potato noodles, beef and broccoli, and won ton soup. As the plates keep coming, I keep hoping that Sylvia will pick up the tab. Will my card accept the charge if I have to split half the bill? I wonder.

"It's nice to be down here in the big city, isn't it?" Sylvia sighs over her plate.

"Yeah, what did they bring you to Vancouver to do?" I ask.

"Oh, I've got a new administrative position. It's really very busy. But my staff is great and I'm loving the office space. Bill and I picked up a new house in Richmond."

"You're kidding. I guess they gave you a bit of a raise with the transfer!"

Sylvia just smiled. Then she started with a little laugh. "So I hear you landed yourself a new job."

"If that is what you call it "I replied. Does she know? Oh, no. Does she know about Subway?

"Subway? Surely Noelle you could do better than that!" It wasn't a question, more like a reprimand.

"I looked everywhere but I ran out of time. I had to find the means to pay the truck payment and Amanda's dance fees".

"Get Amanda to take the job at Subway".

"She can't. She dances six days a week, she needs to do homework, and now with the modeling—there's no spare time in her day."

"Well, how long are you going to work there?"

"Until I can find a better job! Look," I threw up my hands, "I should be so grateful that I have a job at Subway. It beats washing dishes."

"You think?" she smiled, "at least washing dishes nobody can see you."

Ouch. I braced myself under the table and smiled with her.

"Well, no one knows me there. So I don't have to worry about being seen, do I?" She didn't answer. She just shrugged and picked at her plate.

"Sylvia?"

"Yes?"

"How did you know where I was working? I haven't talked to you for months."

She shrugged again and dropped the bomb, "Oh, everybody knows."

Once we got past my employment at Subway, the conversation turned to old times. When the bill came, Sylvia picked up the tab and we made plans to get together again. We hugged and parted ways.

The trip home was painful. I hoped that she was sincere in our parting, that we might still be friends. I needed confirmation that under the sandwich artist, she could still see Noelle, the true and creative woman who used to make our small town dance.

My relief was like spring rain when her email arrived.

Dear Noelle,

Thanks for a fun lunch. It was so nice to spend time with an old friend. I know you are going through a tough time right now, if there is anything I can do to help with your situation, please, let me know.

Sylvia

I cried. And cried. And hoped beyond all hope that I might never have to make that call for help.

There were many more days of sandwich artistry before I found a ray of hope.

Dear God, please help me.

9

Hope came. One afternoon when I got home from work I flipped on the tube. Oprah and a woman named Suze Orman were speaking about Suze's new book, 'Nine Steps to Financial Freedom'. I had never heard of Suze before, but after just a few minutes of watching the show I knew she was a person who would change my world. A woman, telling of her success with Suze as her mentor, said her salary had increased from very little to eight thousand dollars a month in a matter of months. I thought to myself, if this woman can do it so can I. Of course there was doubt too, thinking that this woman was a stockbroker and she had different opportunities than I. We all make excuses for ourselves when we know we are not living to our potential. But even my negative self couldn't dampen my spirits for long. Suze was so inspiring, I wanted what she had. I needed to know what she knew. Elward and I set out to the bookstore that evening and bought the book.

Within days I was a changed person. Or at least, a person set on the road to change. The first seven chapters cover the real money issues; wills, trusts, insurance, debt, retirement plan, investments. Suze explains that you must learn to trust yourself and not someone else with your money. These were all lessons that I needed and I am guessing that since this book was a New York Times Best seller, there were a lot of other people out there in need of the same lessons. It was when I came to chapter seven, eight, and nine that I knew there was a reason I turned to Oprah on that particular day. Twenty-nine pages and my life turned down a different path. Suze answered prayers that I hadn't even prayed! In the last three chapters, those twenty nine pages, she taught me about true wealth and abundance. Not money wealth, but the abundance and wealth of life. She spoke of the natural cycles of money like the tides that flow in and out (this would not be the last time I heard that expression). I learned that as the tides changed so would our money matters, the disappointment and frustration would be replaced with peace and harmony. Why should my life be any different than the up and down swings of the economy?

I loved her "new age" discussion on giving and receiving. I had gone to church a good portion of my life and I knew about tithe, but this was enlightening. The biggest thing that caught my soul, the biggest impact, was when she wrote, *"In order for you to create what is in your power to create, you must believe that you can AND YOU WILL."* It was that day that my life changed because I knew there was hope. I was on my way to being saved

Thank you God for Oprah and Suze Orman!

10

"You must believe that everything that happens is positive, if you are willing to let it be." That's what Suze said, and I wanted to believe. I wanted to let everything be positive. I really tried. Nothing changed for me in the way of income, but I started to change. I greeted the day differently; there was a skip in my step, everything seemed to have a brighter color to it. I was even beginning to appreciate my job at Subway. *Not like, but appreciate.* Life seemed to become livable.

Funny little things started going right. I really tried to follow Suze's advice, to be aware of the details of our finances and that awareness alone helped immensely. Things started coming my way; I found markdowns at the grocery store and coupons that added up to small fortunes. Elward and I celebrated the deals and the blessings as we saw them.

"Can you believe this deal?" I am in the passenger seat of the truck and Elward is driving home a bounteous Safeway harvest.

"Which deal?"

"These sausages. Look Hon, they were on sale, marked down on the package, and then the coupon that was beside them kicked in. Oh, my gosh! Hang on and let me add this up." I run my finger over the receipt and work it out in my head. "No way!"

"What?"

"They actually *paid* us thirty cents to take the sausages home! And check out the total! Three hundred and fifteen dollars turned to one hundred and seventeen after coupons!"

"Well, I'd say that's a pretty good deal there Babe!"

We laughed all the way home. Suze was right. There was money to be found when we started looking. As we made more room for wealth in our lives, money started coming to us. We even received a one thousand dollar check from the damage deposit on an old vehicle lease. The company had forgotten to pay us, and in our crazy, busy world, we had forgotten to ask.

Thanksgiving came and I had a lot to be thankful for. I fought to remember it, to be positive. Everything was positive if I believed it was. It was the most beautiful Thanksgiving we had ever had. Up north there was usually snow on the ground, no leaves on the trees from late August through May, and it was as cold as Christmas, but in Vancouver it was different. The leaves were just beginning to change. Every color and size, from tiny crimson pink to flopping red and gold and crunching chocolate brown. I picked the big beautiful leaves off the ground and made a center piece for the table knowing that I would not be buying one this year. I started to learn to appreciate the simple things, the beauty in nature. It wasn't that I hadn't ever appreciated simple things before, but somehow, in all the turmoil, I had forgotten how.

As an exercise in concentrating on the positive, I wrote a list of everything good in my life.

Full moons over Mt. Baker

Walks in the rain under an umbrella with Elward

Adventures down the tracks to the ocean

The successes of my children

Good health for my family
Our jobs and all that our income provides
    Peaceful thoughts that lead me in a positive direction

I was changing dramatically, but the fact is, my surroundings were not. I was still very heavy, still working at Subway, still struggling to be positive. Elward was still working hard outside through the damp fall weather—about to turn wet and bone aching winter—and our income was still barely enough to live on. When the Thanksgiving charade was over I decided it was time to get real. And Elward got real with me. He calculated the amount of time it would take us to get out from under our debt given our current income and the interest rates that we were paying his father. We never would. We'd be dead first. There had to be more. There just had to.

I felt the door was opening for me. But my body couldn't figure out how to fit through the crack.

Thank you God. Thank you Oprah. Thank you Suze.

11

There had to be more, but what? What would break our financial curse and free us from our debt prison? There was hope for me. Suze said so and I believed it . . . sort of. At least something told me if I could just convince myself that it was true, then it would be. But I didn't believe it. That was the problem. I just plain couldn't make myself believe it. How would I change my mind and my heart to believe that I could be debt free and healthy, even wealthy, when I spent my days making sandwiches and could barely carry the weight of my own body down the street?

Well Reader, for every question asked in prayer, there is an answer, and God heard my question. In response, He sent me a radio ad. It went something like this. . .

'Hello, I'm John Kehoe, author of 'Mind Power into the 21st Century'. Are you tired of struggling with your finances? Do you lack confidence and poise? Are you in debt and out of energy? I have an answer. Let me teach you how to use your mind's power to turn your life around, obtain the life you desire and change your thought patterns forever! I am offering a free seminar this Tuesday and Wednesday night at the Vancouver Hyatt Hotel at seven pm. Come, let me share the secrets of Mind Power with you.'

The next day when I got home from work the radio was on again and as I went to turn it off the same ad ran *again*. I phoned Elward at work and told him about this ad and told him I would like to go listen to this seminar. *Why not? It couldn't hurt to listen.* He encouraged me to go. I planned to go but dinner came and went and I couldn't make myself go. I was afraid.

The next morning as I was serving up a cup of coffee for Elward he came into the kitchen and turned on the radio and *again* the ad played.

"Okay, Elward, that's three times I have heard this ad. I need to go to this seminar."

"Okay. You could have gone last night."

"Hon, do you want to go together?" *Oh, please say yes.* He looked up and saw the *please* in my eyes.

"Sure Babe, we'll make it a date."

That night after a very early dinner we went. It *was* like a date. We took the train, got off at Waterfront and walked up to the Hyatt. It was a beautiful evening. Everything just felt so right! We walked into the Hyatt and my old life flashed in front of me.

I had stayed here many times. I had served as one of the directors on the Hospital Board back home and this was a common place for our meetings. I walked past the doorman and took Elward's arm as we swept past the concierge. Our shoes rang like music on the fine marble floors. Nothing had changed. I looked for the chandeliers on the mezzanine level where the conference halls and ballrooms are. I still loved those magnificent lights dancing through hollow cones of crystal.

"Do you remember those lights?" I said to Elward in a whisper of awe.

"Oh, yes." He smiled. He remembered how much I loved them the time that we stayed here for a week end together in a King suite.

I sighed. "Do you remember Elward? This is how the other half lives."

"I remember."

"I miss it. I miss it so much."

Elward sat in the meeting with me and I was glad that he did because I couldn't have explained this seminar if I had to go home and try. Naturally, Mr. Kehoe did not explain the principles behind all the skills he promised on the radio ad, but he did explain some theory and technique . . . enough to make me want more. And wanting more was the point. Now, to get the rest, I'd have to pay six hundred dollars and take his whole course. I wasn't surprised or offended. To me it wasn't a catch; it was more like a helping hand. I was meant to be there in that room. So once again we pulled out the credit card and used up more of the last dollars available on credit to sign me up for the John Kehoe Mind Power Course. The next time I went, I'd have to go alone.

Thank you God. Thank you Oprah. Thank you Suze. Good to meet you John.

12

I got off the sky train feeling a little nervous and a lot self-conscious. I wanted this class to be everything John Kehoe said it would be. Forget want, I needed it to be. The hotel conference room was cold without Elward beside me. I felt sick. Sick with excitement for what I might learn and sick with fear that there may not be anything here for me after all—that I might have racked up another credit card to pay for a course that would profit me nothing.

I found my seat at the very back of the room and I listened like I had never listened before. I didn't miss a beat; I gobbled it up like a baby eating applesauce. This was the hope I was starving for. By the time the first evening was over I was higher than a kite. I could have self-propelled home with the energy that I absorbed in the meeting. I floated onto the train, sailed into my car, and home. Soaring into the house, I must have been a wonderful sight. Elward looked up from his place on the couch. Then, I said it, out loud—my first mind power truth.

"I will not be working at Subway by Christmas".

"That's my girl." Elward smiled.

I knew in my heart that what I said was true . . . now all I had to do was use John Kehoe's methods to make it so.

Learning Kehoe made me so very aware of my thoughts. I learned that I could not think both positive and negative thoughts at the same time, one pole always dominates, and naturally, the negative prevails. That's the way it is with all of us, we have to choose our thoughts carefully so that positive and productive thoughts can crowd out the negative and destructive ones. *Easier said than done.* As much as I wanted to dig my way out, it would take a lot of practice to change my mind about the way things were.

I became a desperate and dedicated mind power student—knowing now that my return to comfort and health and affluence wasn't just possible—it was already here! I had it all worked out. I had affirmations for weight loss, winning the lottery, making ten thousand dollars a month, improving my state of mind and body. I was consumed in my new found awakening . . . now, if only I could stay awake.

"My subconscious mind and I are partners in success. I am happy, healthy, confident and successful. I weigh one hundred and twenty five pounds and I make ten thousand dollars a month. I won big on the 649. I won so big that I have more money than I will ever need. My subconscious mind and I are partners in success. I am happy, healthy, confident and successful. I weigh one hundred and twenty five pounds and I make ten thousand dollars a month. I won big on the 649. I won so big that I have more money than I will ever need. My subconscious mind and I are partners in success. I am happy, healthy, confident and successful. I weigh one hundred and twenty five pounds and I make ten thousand dollars a month. I won big on the 649. I won so big that I have more money than I will ever need. My subconscious mind and I are partners in success. I am happy, healthy, confident and successful. I weigh one hundred and twenty five pounds and I make ten thousand dollars a month. I won big on the

649. I won so big that I have more money than I will ever need."

And on and on and on. . .listening to tapes and repeating, listening and repeating and slumping in my chair until the warmth of repetition swept up through my legs and over my lungs, drooping me at the shoulders and pulling my eyes closed, bobbing my head on my chest.

I listened and repeated all day long. Before work, at work, in the line at the bank and the meat isle of the grocery store.

"All my needs are met. I am always in the right place at the right time. There are no coincidences. All my needs are met. I am always in the right place at the right time. There are no coincidences. All my needs are met. I am always in the right place at the right time. There are no coincidences. All my needs are met. I am always in the right place at the right time. There are no coincidences. I am always in the right place at the right time. There are no coincidences All my needs are met. I am always in the right place at the right time. There are no coincidences. All my needs are met."

Before bed, in bed, any time, all the time, if I could be affirming, I was. And it was exhausting. I fell asleep sitting up, lying down, even leaning on the wall. Like a moth trapped in a chandelier, the warmth of repetition and the flicker of hope lulled me to a state of barely aware. I was in a mind power trance.

Thank you God. Tha. . . zzzzzzzzzzzzzzzzzz

13

"I can't keep this up, Elward, I'm napping everywhere."

"Maybe you are just coming down from all the stress."

"Yeah, well, it feels good to come down y'know."

"Sure, but is all the repetition doing any good if you are sleeping through it?"

I had to face it, sleeping my way through the day was relaxing, but it didn't feel like it was getting me anywhere, so, I had to step it up a notch. I started writing. I call this time in my healing and learning 'Kehoe Kindergarten' because that is just what it was. Like a kid writing lines, I wrote my affirmations.

My subconscious mind and I are partners in success. My subconscious mind and I are partners in success. My subconscious mind and I are partners in success. My subconscious mind and I are partners in success. My subconscious mind and I are partners in success. My subconscious mind and I are partners in success. My subconscious mind and I are partners in success. My subconscious mind and I are partners in success. My subconscious mind and I are partners in success. My subconscious mind and I are partners in success.

And on and on until I would slump over my pen and Elward would lay me onto the bed.

It was like I was a kid all over again. My mother and father demanded that we never say "Shut Up!", and every time one of us got caught saying it, my father would make us write lines. I remember sitting at the table writing many times, *I must not say shut up I must not say shut up*, over and over and over again. Pages of *I must not say shut up*.

As awkward as the method may have been, the results started to show. The whole family got in on it. Amanda and I would make a game of catching each other in the act of negative self talk.

"I am way too fat." I mutter in the bathroom mirror.

"I heard that." Amanda peaks through the open door. "Now, was that positive?"

"I thought I was alone in here."

"Nope, never alone, you always have your subconscious and if that's not enough, I'll be hanging around here listening!" She grins and passes by the door with a wink.

She wants to keep me on track. My new attitude must be such a relief to her. Elward is a great support too. He keeps the house quiet while I am writing, giving endless excuses on the phone to keep me sheltered from interruption. He believes in me and he believes that this is very possible, that if there is help to be had we need all the help we can get. But was it really helping? My attitude was changing, but even my first mind power statement had not yet been fulfilled.

Thank you God. Thank you Oprah. Thank you Suze. Thank you John?

14

Kehoe's classes were coming to an end. I was positive, I was strong, I was ready to take on the world and I was sick to death of Subway. But there was no light at the end of the sandwich tunnel. Christmas was just around the corner and I was still slapping sandwiches together in my charcoal pants and visor. My first mind power truth was about to fall flat on its proverbial face. And then . . .

"Oh, my gosh, Elward, I am sick. I am so damned sick." Elward rolls over in bed to touch my face.

"What the . . . Noelle, you are burning up!"

"What will I do? My last Kehoe session is tonight."

"Sorry Babe, you won't be goin'"

"I guess I'd better call in sick to Subway too."

"Better do."

I loved making the Subway call. Any time off from there seemed like a good idea, but now we'd be short of money, and just before Christmas.

The cough got worse through the day and the fever did not break. I heaved on the bed and shivered on the couch and soaked in the tub, but to no avail. All the positive thinking on earth would not end the pain in my chest and when I finally gave in and went to the hospital, they couldn't believe I had stayed away so long.

"Good grief," the doctor says as he listens to my chest and lungs. "Another day like this and you'd have suffocated in your sleep. You've got enough infection in those lungs to kill you three times over!"

I came out of the hospital a week later well practiced in my mantras, but doubting just the same. How could I have been affirming health and still end up in the hospital half dead?

The day I got out of hospital, my boss called and asked why I was not at work. "I just got out of the hospital," I said.

"Well I figured you would be better by now."

"Not quite, but thanks for asking."

"Well, we made up the schedule for next week."

"Oh?"

"Yes, we have you on the day shift for the Tuesday, Wednesday and Friday, Saturday."

"Friday is Christmas day."

"Yes. You are on the schedule for that day."

I took the leap and shared my first mind power statement with my boss. "I won't be working at Subway for Christmas."

There was a long silence. Then his voice again, but it was tight and throttled. "What do you mean you won't be working at Christmas."

"I won't be working on Christmas day, in fact, I won't be back. I am not well enough to come in for at least another week and I am giving you my notice. I won't be back, not today, not tomorrow, not at all."

"Oh."

"So, thank you for the opportunity you gave me to work for you." *I can't get this smile off my face.*

"Yes, well, it was nice having you work here." He is stunned.

"Have a good day then."

"Yes, and you too." He hung up.

I sat on the couch and waited for Elward to come home. I would tell him I was jobless. He would understand. I waited on the couch for a few hours, and the longer I waited, the more concerned I got. Jobless, and a week before Christmas. This was not good. That's not what I intended when I set my mind to be out of Subway. What I intended was to not have to work there . . . to have a better option by then. I didn't have time to worry for long, because my phone rang again.

"Hello?"

"Hi, Aunt Noelle? This is Michael."

"Hi. How's my favorite nephew?"

"I'm great. How are you feeling? I've been worried about you."

"I'm good. I just quit my job at Subway."

"Really? You know, I heard that the company I used to work for is hiring now. Y'know when I was helping out with that group home—all those troubled kids. You should send in a resume right away and I'll put in a word for you."

"Well, I've worked with a *few* youth in my day. This might really be a great idea. Thanks Michael. I'll get my resume together today."

I faxed over a cover letter and my resume and they called back that day to invite me for an interview. Then I found ads for two other agencies that were looking for care givers and applied to them as well. Within two days I had three interviews and was offered three jobs. I chose the one Michael recommended. It was close to home with a great working arrangement. I was assigned to a teenage girl who was struggling with a heroin addiction. The arrangement wasn't perfect. It would keep me sleeping away from home a few nights a week, but even still, it was a miracle for me. My income had doubled and I felt like I was making a difference in the world. I had helped a lot of young girls to improve. Why not Arina?

With the assurance of a great job on the horizon, Christmas was a real celebration. Brock came home from his US Tour, LJ and his fiancé returned from their contract in Japan, and Amanda was thrilled to have everyone back together. The snow fell hard for two days and so, our coastal Christmas turned white, and we all felt like we were at home. For those few days, I stopped asking through mantras and just said *Thank You* for everything I have been given.

Thank you God. Thank you Oprah. Thank you Suze. Thank you John.

15

Working with Arina started the second week of January. I was well again and feeling very positive. A miracle had happened for me. And I learned something when I realized that I had to take the step to show I believed before the full answer came my way. I had to quit Subway before the call from Michael came. I would remember this lesson. It would make me a woman who could step out in faith believing that God heard my prayers and that there was power in my thoughts.

On working days, I spent my days doing mantras and my nights with Arina. On my days off, I spent my days doing mantras and my nights living a family life in the truest sense of the word. In my old life, in twenty five years of marriage, I had never made a dinner for the family during the week. I had never been home when my children got home from school, let alone my husband from work. Now, although I only got to do it for three or four nights a week, I loved this new way of living. I thought, 'So this is how the normal people lived.' Dinner at 5:30 and a walk at night, rain or shine, with my man. I cherished every moment.

LJ married in February and we didn't have a penny to help with the wedding. We only made it there because we pulled out our last stashed credit card. It was a beautiful wedding. They were married in the chapel at the Bellagio in Las Vegas. String quartet and the whole nine yards. I had to apologize to the father of the bride. *Sorry we couldn't help with the wedding costs.*

That was a tough one I'll tell you. For me to know that I didn't have money was one thing, but to have to tell my son's new father-in-law that we didn't have any money was another all together.

For two months after the wedding I kept on asking, confirming, affirming that I was secure financially, confident, successful.

At the end of April my phone rang and an old friend was on the other end.

"Hi, Noelle, it's Kelly."

"Kelly? I haven't heard from you since forever!"

"I know. We really ought to be better about staying in touch."

"Yeah, that would be good. How are you doing?"

"Really well. I suppose you are a great as ever?" she said.

"Oh, yeah, things are fabulous, I love living here on the coast."

"Hmmm, it's nice. Say, I have a friend who is taking over a studio in your area. She's new to this and looking for a few great instructors. I told her you were in the area and she flipped! She's really hoping you'll come over. It would help her kick off the studio on the right foot y'know? So I said I'd call you and make the pitch for her."

"What's the pitch?"

"Ballet and tap, thirty dollars per hour."

"Thirty?" Omigosh, thirty dollars and hour, that's at least another two thousand dollars a month!

"Yeah, I told her that's not really enough for someone like you, but she's just starting out and. . ."

"I know, I understand. Tell her to give me a call and I'll meet with her at her studio. I'll go for thirty."

"Oh, hey, thanks Noelle, it will mean a lot to her to have your name on the roster."

We chatted awhile and when I hung up the phone I danced. I really danced.

Thank you God. Thank you Oprah. Thank you Suze. Thank you John.

16

The first day of classes at the studio was a bit of a shock. Of course I connected well with the students. Of course. But the parents who did not know dance or my reputation in it were expecting something different when I walked into the room. There it was again, that head to toe look over, and then one mother actually blurted it out.

"That's her? You have got to be kidding me!"

It was no joke. Nope, I wasn't kidding. And by the end of the first few classes they knew why I had dancers all over the world in the finest shows and on the most famous stages. I still knew my stuff.

To make the new schedule work, I made a request to the childcare company. "Please let Arina come and live in our home so she can see how normal families live." They agreed and I thought it was fine. Now I'd be getting double employment while still living in my new normal world. Teaching was different than owning the place. I was relaxed, I was gaining health and I was getting sleep. I was getting plenty of sleep, but my Amanda was not . . .

"Noelle, . . . Noelle."

"Hmmm Mmmm."

"Wake up Hon, just for a second."

"Hmmmm, yeah?"

"Honey. I got up for work and went out for a coffee. . . Amanda is still up watching T.V.

"What?" I push up from the bed. "That's the third time this week she's been up all night."

"I know." Elward's voice is filled with worry. "I'll talk to her and see what is going on."

Amanda didn't have much to say about being up all night except that her joints hurt and she couldn't sleep. I didn't get it. Everyone can sleep. Just lie down and close your eyes and stop fretting. *Just go to sleep! Stop watching the stinking television and get to bed!*

My logic got us nowhere. The lack of sleep continued and soon came the headaches and the chills, and the pain in her joints just got worse and worse until finally. . .

Amanda comes in the door, the cool fall air pushing past her as she stumbles over the step—crumbling onto the floor.

"Are you okay?" I come around the corner to see what the commotion is. I reach for her and she accepts my hand. She picks herself up, shuffles to the couch and falls again. There are tears. A flood of tears like I have never seen before.

"Sweetie, what is it?"

"I can't dance. I have to stop. I need canes. I can't do this any more. No more!"

"What do you mean?"

"Mom, it's the pain. I've been trying to tell you. It's been months. It's so terrible. I can't live like this anymore. It's so *terrible*. It goes through every joint. It's in my hips. Oh, my hips!"

I hold her and bring her ice. When Elward came home we took her to the doctor.

"She won't dance again—she has fibromyalgia. And I think you might consider that bipolar and depression often go along with fibromyalgia. The drugs I'm prescribing will treat mood and pain." he said.

There's got to be another answer. I'm not drugging my daughter.

It was time to call my brother Tony, again.

"Has she been taking the supplement?" he asked.

"Yes, we think so." I said.

"How often, and how much?"

I made a guess and even if I guessed high, it wasn't enough.

Tony recommended an increase and a more regular use of the supplement and the magic began once again. Just like the first time, her symptoms began to subside. She started sleeping and within a couple of months, she was dancing as though the pain had never been there.

The day she came home asking for canes was her last day of classes. Now, having quit class, she wanted to go off on her own and dance professionally. I would not hold her back. She would work her way back to health and I would help her.

With my last dancer planning to leave home, I needed to reassess my own interest in dance. I could see that the studio would not do well and I was becoming very unhappy with the management. I would set rules in my class and the owner would change them back. She didn't want advice, she didn't want suggestions. She wasn't interested in my experience.

I decided that I would not return the next season and the studio went belly up before the next season finished. I never felt like a loser or a quitter, I just knew that I was an expert in my field, and this field was about to be closed down for lack of fans.

Now, down a good chunk of income, I wasn't really worried. I still cared for Arina and I had learned from all of my mentors that there would be another opportunity if I would ask for it. And I was still asking, still affirming my success, my wealth, my confidence.

And I was buying my lottery tickets. Still grateful for all those who had gone before and were willing to share the secrets of their success with me.

Thank you God. Thank you Oprah. Thank you Suze. Thank you John.

17

In February of 2000 I kept getting this vibration. It was like something was coming. Like a train in the distance, I could feel it through my feet. I could feel it rushing toward me in the air.

"Can you feel it Elward?" We are sitting at the dinner table, mulling over a couple plates of pasta.

"Feel what?"

"The air, it's different. Something has changed. Something really good is coming our way."

"What is it?"

"I don't know. I'll know when it gets here." Elward just smiles. By now he was willing to believe me when I say the air is different. We will wait together to see what change is on the way.

A few nights later, I went downstairs to do some online banking.

"Elward! Elward come here!" He came quickly and we both stood staring at the screen a little shocked and happy to be hit by that train I had felt coming. Our very old and stagnant trading account had risen from the dead.

In a moment I had a new job. In our old life, Elward had been doing some commodities and trading, and he was very good at it. He understood how the market worked. I asked him to teach me the ins and outs of trading. I started buying and selling and keeping an eye on it all day long. And I got to be pretty good at it. Elward found me a chat room for day traders and I began to follow their stocks. He signed me up for instant quotes, called "Real Time" so I could see exactly how the stocks were valued at any moment without the average 15 minute delay. Things were going very well. I was beginning to make money at this.

In April, Elward and I received stocks from our life insurance company that had gone public. This was a nice bonus. We sold them and added the money to our trading fund. Our trading account was now high enough that we would be able to buy larger price tag stocks or more quantity of the lower priced stocks.

I was really enjoying this, and it consumed my day. I researched interesting stocks, bought and sold, and knew that this is what I would use to replace my teaching income.

In May, auditions for Tokyo Disney came up in California. Arina was too sick to come along and so I made new arrangements for her. Now, it was just me and my girl.

Amanda and I went to LA together—just the two of us. We had the time of our lives! We went to Venice beach, had key tags made with our pictures on them, dined out, walked around the shops, and just really enjoyed each other. The same day of the audition Amanda was awarded a position. She would go in the fall. Her dance career was back on its feet for good! We celebrated by going to Disneyland for the night.

When we came home, Arina was gone for good. She had gotten into the heroine again and back into prostitution to pay for her drugs. The agency had put her into a protective rehab; a women's care facility to protect her from herself and any current clientele.

I was sad for Arina, but I knew that my life had turned a corner. It was time for me to take on full time day trading. Life was changing for me . . . and all for the better.

Thank you God. Thank you Oprah. Thank you Suze. Thank you John.

18

Every morning I woke up, got Elward out the door and got straight onto my computer. I had some really good days and some not so good days but I was learning the ropes and turning out way more good than bad. One morning before eight o'clock I had made just less than twenty thousand on Corel and the next day I bought in again and made some more.

Things were going great. So great that I got my Fridays back! As soon as the stock market closed for the day, I was out the door. I spent my Fridays in the spa or the salon; I'd walk in the affluent neighborhoods and invite a friend out for lunch. I was back! I was working hard and I was a success. I was living the good life. I was on my way to making myself a millionaire.

I started seeing an old friend, a hairdresser from up North. She had moved down to Vancouver too and was working in a really posh salon—the kind smart day traders could afford. Mike was a beautiful woman of European descent. She was tall and noble looking with light eyes and strong blonde hair. I loved to go to her for my hairdo. It was always a good conversation.

"You are looking well Noelle." Mike is parting my hair and wrapping chunks in foil for my color.

"Thanks, I'm doing fantastic."

"How is your family?"

"Oh, everyone is fabulous. The kids are dancing and Elward is loving his job."

"How are things going for you with the day trading?"

"I'm acing this thing Mike. I mean some days are better than others, but I'll tell you, I cannot lose! You know last week with Corel I pulled in over twenty grand . . . but this week I'm *only* up about fifteen hundred."

She set my hair down and put a hand on my shoulder. Then looking at me through the mirror she said, "You aren't getting greedy are you?"

She didn't get it. It wasn't called greed, it was called success and I was having success. I asked for it. I used my mind power to take what was mine in the universe and I deserved every penny of it.

It's called success. And I earned it.

One night, after a very successful day trading, the phone rang. I rolled over in bed to pick it off the lamp table and checked the caller ID. It was my brother Tony.

"Hello?"

"Oh, hi Noelle, I hope it's not too late to call you, I was just thinking about you and wanted to give you a call."

"No, Tony, it's okay. I'm in bed but let's talk."

"Yeah, good, well I wanted see how it's going for you. How's Amanda?"

"We just got an email from her in Japan, she loves it there and things are going really well!"

"Aww, that's great eh? Good on ya." I could hear the smile in my brother's voice. Another success not unlike the success he had had with his own daughter. It made him happy, so happy to take his painful experience and turn it into something beautiful for other people. "Say, have you got a minute?" he asked.

"Sure Tony, what's up?"

"Things are going really well for the company and we are getting some decent publicity now. David and I can't keep personally supporting all of these people and when the magazine article comes out, we'll be over our heads. We need to set up some call centers to develop a support system. Do you want to take that on out there in Vancouver? You'd be able to handle a lot of people on your own and when it gets to be too much, you could have Elward or somebody come help out. Y'know with Amanda getting better twice on this, you could really help some people with your story."

I am silent.

"Hey? What do you think?" He is hopeful.

"No, we are doing really well with the trading and Elward likes his job, he just loves working outdoors. Thanks for thinking of us though Tony. I hope it's a great success for you."

He wouldn't drop the request. "We are doing a meeting out there in a couple weeks, do you want to come?"

I said no. Elward said yes. I just wasn't interested. In fact, after the way the trading went today, and the celebration Elward and I enjoyed over a steak dinner, I knew that the path of trading that I was on, was the only path I would need.

I stayed home when Elward went to check out Tony's business. Elward came home and said he wished I had come with him. It was good. Tony was making sense. Maybe we should get involved. I didn't want Tony's path. I had my own.

I created this path. It was mine to follow. The market was hot and at the rate I was going, we would have our debt paid off and would be able to retire; living the lifestyle I asked for in no time at all.

It's called success. I created it, I earned it. It's mine.

19

Over the year Tony had called me three times to ask me to help him. And three times, I said no. Three times. Then, one morning, God came knocking on my door . . .

Summer had faded into fall and with Amanda and Brock overseas, the house seemed naked. I spent the days alone with my money, typing and sending, buying, selling and researching. Elward spent his days building and creating. Our evenings were ours alone. It was quiet.

"Do you feel it Elward?" We are on the couch with a bag of microwave popcorn and a television for company.

"Feel what?"

"I don't know. It's like a train in the distance . . . but it doesn't feel good."

"Never mind Honey, it's just with the kids gone . . . you are lonely."

The next morning when I checked my stocks, things were not looking good. The Science and Tech market was falling apart and I had a lot of Science and Tech stocks. I went upstairs and grabbed a bowl of cereal. I sat at the table and made it half way through the cereal before the sickest feeling came over me. I couldn't finish the cereal. I dropped my spoon and put my head on the table and started to cry. Uncontrollable floods of tears and gut wrenching sadness filled my body and choked my throat. I wanted my Elward to come home, I wanted my children to come home, and I did not want to stay in this house alone.

I needed out. What was my problem? I was happy for my children. I did not really want them to come home but without them, the family pattern was broken. When one of us was down, the others held him up. It seemed we always had taken turns being down and lifting the other up. Who was going to hold me up now?

Now the market had been rough for about a week. But that wasn't new—like the ocean tide I had come to know so well, markets ebb and flow and over the period of a day or three, there is a natural pattern to things. I had learned this and so, a small loss here and there was expected and accepted. It was only a part of the world I had chosen to be in. I kept telling myself that. Kept writing about it, affirming support and stability in my investments but, as the week went on, the shallow tide of wealth kept slipping and the ebb and flow quickly became only flow. Like sand through my fingertips, all of my investments were falling through. I felt a darkness creeping over me. I didn't think it could get worse than this. *Could it?*

I woke up with a feeling of confidence. Today would be the day that all of this would turn around. I just knew it. Elward was already at work and so, I'd eat breakfast in front of the computer. I checked my status and bit my toast. Things hadn't changed. I was still on the losing end everywhere. I needed to get things moving. I found a stock that looked safe and put down all my chips. This was surely what I needed to do to turn things around. It felt right and I needed to get every part of me on board with that right feeling, so I slipped on my shoes and left.

I'd walk the beach for awhile, speaking my affirmations all the way along the promenade. I started back feeling centered and peaceful and capable once more.

On the promenade, I would do a visual affirmation. As I walked I would speak, but I would look like a person speaking to myself. So, as people approached I would stop moving my lips and continue the affirmation in my mind. I spoke *I am healthy, happy, confident and successful.* I would visualize healthy like the man on the Excedrin bottle surrounded with energy, happy—me laughing in a group of people, confident—me in business clothes in front of a group of people, successful—I am writing a check to Elward's Dad. I am free of the burden of debt . . . then I would go on, *I make ten thousand dollars a month*—I would see myself paying all of my bills. *I weigh one hundred and twenty five pounds*—visualize myself small, firm, sexy. *I won big on the six-forty-nine . . . so big that I have more money than I will ever need!* And I see myself a winner going into the store where I bought the ticket. I see myself from above—winning. *Winning big!*

I'll be okay, because that's how it works—ask and receive. Step up and take what is yours. I was one of the smart ones. I had it all figured out. I was one of the few who really got it. *Ask and ye shall receive right?*

I won big. I won so big. Why? Because I said so.

20

I was gone only an hour. My walk on the beach, sauntering and affirming success on the promenade was only for one hour. One hour. And it was over. The flicker of the computer monitor flung horror into my face as I realized what was going on. Everybody was bailing out and I tried too. I typed and sent, typed and sent, enter... enter...enter...I couldn't tap the keyboard fast enough. The price just kept dropping. Twenty to eighteen, fourteen . . .

"No please."
seven fifty,
"No, dammit, no. Stop! Stop!"
six, five, four and a quarter,
"Oh, No!"
four, three.

I slam my keyboard and sink into the back of my chair. Then, the thought of telling Elward what I had done sweeps me and I fall from my chair onto the floor.

When he came in the door, hours later, the carpet was wet with my tears and I was in a ball of hysteria, mumbling something of "it's all gone, it's all gone. I want it back."

Oh God, please, bring it back. Give it back to me.

When I realized Elward was home, my mumbles turned to wails. He sat on the floor next to me and let me cry until there were no tears left. When I could speak, I poured out my heart to him.

"Oh, Elward, I'm so sorry, I didn't do my job. I lost everything and I thought that would never happen."

"Hon, it happened to a lot of people today. It's okay." That's what he said, but his eyes gave him away. His wheels were turning. What would we do? We had been planning our retirement around that money, our livelihood and our whole future. He was as devastated as I was. He had to be.

Watching the news, I came to understand that I was not the only one affected. Pension plans, life savings, homes, futures, everything was affected but it did not make it any easier for me to handle. It felt very personal to me. It felt like it was intended only for me . . . the train in the distance had bowled right over my signpost of success.

I was sick, really sick. Something inside of me clicked and I was not the same person. I despised the morning. I would stay in bed and let the tears, hot, bitter, broken tears, run down my face. I didn't want to wake up. I wanted death. Eventually I would get up and go through the motions.

Sometimes in the middle of the day I would get so desperate that I'd just have to pick up the phone.

"Elward?" I'd speak even before he could say hello.

"Hi, are you okay?"

"No. I'm not." The tears would choke my words and I'd let go. I'd wail and he'd have to step away from his co-workers so they couldn't hear through the cell. "I'm not okay. It's going to kill me. This pain is too much. What have I done? What have I done!" There wasn't much to say. He'd get home as soon as he could and find me on the couch holding the life insurance papers flipped to the page on payout for death by suicide. He'd shake his head and cry and beg me not to let this take me.

Things will get better. Things will get better.

Oh, Reader, it was dark, this time in my life. It seemed to me that everything I had worked for, everything I thought I had was gone. I had convinced myself that I had what I did because of something that I did . . . and in an hour it was gone. Adding to that the personal grief, Elward's broken relationship with his father, the guilt I felt was immense. Adding to that the loneliness . . . the empty nest feeling, when the three people I had formed my whole life around were gone. Oh, it was lonely. I had no purpose here and in my darkest nights, I could hear the whisper; *Elward is slim and smooth and fit. He is good looking and everything that he would need to be to find another woman; a better, smarter, lovelier woman. He deserves better than you. It would be a favor. Go on. Do him a favor. Do it for Elward. Do it. Save him from a life time of living with you.*

The darkness came. And Elward stayed. And I gave no thanks.

21

Elward cashed in the pittance that was left of our stocks, the ones worth selling, and tallied up the damages. All told, we could make it through to the end of January before we'd be bankrupt. He said if I believed in a merciful God, then now might be the time to put in a word.

Before the market crashed, I had picked up a book called '*The Power of Your Subconscious Mind,*' by Joseph Murphy. I didn't know why I picked it up—everything was going my way back then, and the skills I had learned from Kehoe seemed to be enough for me. But now, in my newfound desperation, I picked up the book and began to read it. There was a section in there about a man who needed to improve his thought pattern since he was always telling himself that he would never have enough. Murphy came up with a way to solve it. So I hoped and prayed that if it worked for this man then it would work for me. Murphy, unlike Kehoe used the words of the Bible in his writings. I found comfort in those words and I believed. These familiar refrains I had learned on my own father's knee taught me once again, not only about asking and receiving, but also about gratitude and thanksgiving. I knew that I was going to be healed if I did what he recommended.

And so it went. Every time I would get a run of anxiety or thoughts of suicide or lack I would invoke Mr. Murphy's help and focus on asking for the positive answer to my negative self. Murphy taught me that every time you get the thoughts in your mind, the ones that should not be there, you have to ask for them to be removed. I asked and received. I would ask every time that I got anxious, sad, or sorry, pointing out to God that there couldn't be room for thoughts like these in my mind and asking Him to clear it and allow only healing thoughts in my head. Slowly, I got over the anxiety. Slowly I stopped thinking those thoughts and they just went away—*until the next time*. I struggled with sudden tears and overwhelming sadness. I battled and thought it away day after long day until Elward finally gave me the answer.

"Y'know, Amanda left a half bottle of the supplement up in the cupboard." Elward's statement sounds like a question.

"Yeah? That was silly, we ought to send it to her."

"Or, maybe, if you want to, you could take it?"

"Elward. I don't have a mood problem . . . this is *real*."

"Maybe, but I think it can't hurt to try." He got up from the table, grabbed the bottle and poured six capsules into his hand. "Please Babe. Just try it for me."

I would do anything for Elward. Anything. Even if it meant taking a supplement that was meant for depressed people, when I was justified in my depression. He kept feeding it to me and I was functional again in only three days. I felt myself healing. It was a miracle! I now had enough clarity in my mind to deal with the issues at hand. I was no longer suicidal. No. Now I was on a mission and Joseph Murphy and God were going to help me get through this.

I went back to doing affirmations and mantras, but now it was not like a self-hypnosis as much as it was like prayer. I started every day in prayer and then stepped into my private place every half hour through the day to pray again. Every prayer was accompanied by a mental movie—a visualization that helped me to stay on track and move it along. Joseph Murphy taught me that I didn't need to be afraid to ask for what I wanted because it was never the Lord's desire to have poverty, lack, or negativity in our lives. He did not give us this, we created it ourselves, and He is sad when he sees us suffering.

There were many videos I played in my head as I asked God to bring me abundance and help me to meet my needs. But my favorite is the one where, as I asked for abundance, I saw myself in the street.

I am a dancer again, small and strong and graceful. I am healthy, I am happy, I am noble. I am reaching to the sky, twirling around and around in the middle of a quiet street. God is sending a rainfall of blessings. Light and rich, they cascade over me like golden confetti, drifting and eventually heaping at my feet.

Oh, thank you God. Thank you for Elward and my children, thank for the likes of Oprah and Suze, and wise men like Joseph Murphy. Thank you.

22

As time moved along the finances didn't improve but the state of my mind did and that was the most important thing ever. I came to understand that there was a lesson or two in the crash. I had become cocky, self absorbed and yes, greedy. I loved the stock market. I loved the money. The power of the trade. The thrill of the win. In my greed I was not becoming the person God intended me to be. I was never cut out to be selfish or cold. I was created to be generous and kind.

Tony called me one more time and asked for my help in setting up meetings for Truehope in British Columbia. This time, I said yes, and Elward smiled.

At the meeting, I met a woman who said she had gone from psychotic to well using Tony's supplement. Her minister was so pleased. He had spent a lot of time counseling her. The congregation had spent so much energy praying for her. The minister asked her to see if the men from Truehope would come and talk to a group of ministers at a regional convention. *Of course they would.*

The meeting was planned for December. Even though I was trying to help Tony, there really wasn't any money in it for me. We were still in trouble. We were going under.

I went to praying hourly. I set the kitchen timer and took ten minutes out of every hour to have prayers. But it did not change the inevitable.

Brock was in trouble too, his show had ended a little earlier than 'planned' and he was out of work. Some personalities are prone to mischief and Brock was one of those personalities! I probably should have been upset at him for being sent home before his contract was over, but I was so glad to see him that I couldn't muster any motherly indignation. We enjoyed a few weeks together, walking on the beach and clearing my head and his. I supported him and he supported me and then I told him it was time for us to get back to the real world and start working and living again.

When Brock landed another job on a cruise ship, I took him to the docks to say good bye. I watched him go as he walked on to the ship, his guitar slung over one shoulder and his bag of homemade cookies in the other hand. He turned to wave good-bye, and I cried. I loved him, my youngest boy. I shook my head and wiped my tears and smiled as I watched him go. His mischievous side was something he never grew out of and it was bound to get him in real trouble one of these days.

Brock's leaving got me crying and the crying just wouldn't stop! I sat in the car for an hour shedding the stress that I had bottled so well when my boy was home. I didn't want to worry him, so Elward and I had said nothing about our impending bankruptcy.

I got home from the docks and collapsed at the kitchen table. I prayed into the table top for an hour or more. Give me strength, bring me the wealth I need, take these terrible thoughts from me and provide a way to get out of this financial mess without going bankrupt.

When Elward came home I was still at the table.

"You know, if we wait until the bankruptcy, we won't have a chance to see LJ in his new home." I said.

"I know." He sat down next to me.

"If we are going to go down completely, why don't we just speed up the inevitable and get out there to see LJ now, while we still can?"

Elward smiled and we started planning the trip.

A couple weeks into December, the ministerial meeting was held. Tony and David were great. The excitement and the interest from the ministers made me proud to be a part of this new movement. While at the meeting the same woman who asked for the ministers meeting offered to host a meeting for her entire community church. I said I'd love to plan one for January. From a meeting like that, I'd be able to start supporting people who wanted to use the supplement, and that is where the money would start coming for me. Would it come quickly enough?

We took what was left of our stock money and with some help from our remaining credit cards went to see LJ for Christmas. And, for Christmas, I was given a wonderful gift. Joseph Murphy's second book called, *Your Infinite Power to be Rich*. And another gift—I found a horoscope that said "*A big surprise is coming your way.*"

I was so ready for a good surprise.

In this new book, I found a new way of approaching prayer with finer examples of positive living and a deeper understanding of how to use words to express my faith and intentions. The entire book was about situations. His experiences with people, their situations and the prayers that they used to achieve the manifestation they desired.

Christmas was short, but beautiful. We loved spending time with our oldest boy. It's nice, when your kids are grown and you can enjoy them as adults. It's a beautiful thing to have intelligent conversations and to teach, and be taught by someone you raised. Seeing LJ was a break that was so needed—away from thoughts of being broke.

All the way home, my mind battled with the thoughts of our impending bankruptcy, so I delved into my new book searching for answers and for peace.

"Hey, Elward, get this. Joseph says that direction and answers can come to you from God in any place you are likely to be looking. Writings, scripture, newspapers, even horoscopes."

"Well, of course."

"Even horoscopes? What do you think of that?"

"Hon," he said, "If you believe that God is omnipotent and omnipresent, then why would He not put your answers where you are most likely to find them?"

"I'm learning so much Elward, and I have faith that there is an answer for us. Maybe I'm just not looking in the right places."

"Well, we'll just have to keep looking, I guess."

We got home and scrounged what we could together in the way of credit card advances. For the month, we didn't pay our bills. There had to be a way out of this. I asked, and affirmed, and prayed.

I went out and picked up the newspaper and brought it in. I opened to the horoscope and there was my answer. It read:

So, you are going back into childcare. Good for you. But don't worry; it won't last longer than six months.

Why hadn't I thought of this before? I got up and phoned my old boss and asked if she had a child for me to care for. Within a week, Stanley was in our house. And I was making just under four thousand dollars a month caring for him—a sweet boy who had been diagnosed as a psychopath.

We didn't file for bankruptcy after all and I offered an extra prayer of thanksgiving.

Thank you God for everything. Thank you for knowing where your answer for me would be found. Thank you for Oprah and Suze, John and Joseph. Yes, thanks so much for Joseph.

23

Stanley was a psychopath . . . literally. The tests proved it. They called him a socialized psychopath. He was charming; a sweet talker with a look of pure innocence. He had a shallow build, pointed elbows and frail wrists. Light hair, light eyes, a lovely full-lipped smile. I thought they were wrong. They had to be. I put him on the Truehope supplements and saw massive improvement in him, his school work, concentration, even his sleep improved, I fell in love with the little guy, but it didn't take long before the honeymoon ended. By week three, Stanley was everything they said he was. He manipulated and threatened and stared like a wiccan drawing up a wretched curse on my head. By week four, I was convinced he was a murder waiting to happen, but I wanted so badly to help this boy.

I wanted to see him become well and live up to his potential. Stanley truly was God's gift to me. Not only for income, but also for preparation for what was to come. I was learning patience and tolerance and I was learning how to know when enough was enough and when it was okay to give up.

Living with Stanley made me think of all the people who are sick and can actually be helped with the things my brother knew—the Truehope Program. I started thinking about Truehope, my brother, and his request for help. I started thinking that maybe there was more to the request than just the offer of a job. Why had he been so persistent when I had turned him down cold the first time? Why hadn't I seen it? Twice Amanda had seen a full recovery from illness and stress using Tony's supplement. Twice she had avoided trading her career for a bottle of drugs. And I had seen a miracle in my own life. Truly, a miracle of healing—it ended my anxiety, quieted my suicidal thoughts and calmed me to the center of my soul at a time when everything else had failed me. Was it time for me to be giving back? *Of course.* God knew my potential to do good and when I was so blinded by my blessings he simply came knocking on my door and said: *Say, you don't mind if I borrow this money for a while until you humble yourself do you?*.

Had I needed every part of that experience? Even to the point of humility, pain and anguish? Even sorrow, despair, suicidal desire and obsession? Yes, yes, yes. I needed all of that. Every miserable bit.

I humbled myself and committed myself to do my part, I would work for Truehope.

24

Tony had welcomed me with open arms and gave me all of the training he could come up with to get me ready to offer support for others. Then I talked a couple of reporters into writing some stories about Truehope's success in Alberta. We put on the meeting for the church congregation and I made it known in the community that I would be representing Truehope in the Vancouver and Washington area. As the financial relief poured in with Stanley, people came out of the woodwork looking for help through Truehope.

The lectures were fantastic. I went home every time with a new resolve to be healthy and to help others to be healthy. I worked for months developing the support program in my area. I set up many more lectures and my brother and David came to speak. Very quickly, I had four hundred participants and I supported them through the decision to try the Truehope program. I talked to their doctors and explained the theory behind the success of the supplement. I talked on the phone to participants in the early morning, all day, and into the evening—but I remembered to take time to talk to myself too. I loved it. I truly loved my work. When the work became too much to handle, I set a mantra and asked for the perfect person to come and work with me in the office. I happened to send out a request to an employment agency and that same day Tessa called, she was perfect in every way. It didn't take long before I realized that Tessa's life experiences presented her with the tools to do this job. I loved her and so did my clients. We were a team. When it got too big for Tessa and me to handle, Elward dedicated his evenings to helping me in the office .... just like Tony had suggested he would.

Exactly six months after Stanley arrived, the agency tried to take him away. I could have let him go and it would have been the fulfillment of the horoscope that brought him to me in the first place, but I fought to keep him. I was so sure that I'd be able to help him, even that he would be healed. The agency gave in and agreed to have him stay. Although they made a point of saying that they had never had anyone fight to keep any child before, let alone Stanley. I was thankful for the chance to make a difference in Stanley's life. Helping others had become a true mission for me. I struggled to help him for months, but as summer faded into fall again, Stanley was making no marked improvements.

Thanksgiving Holiday was on the way and the leaves were turning again. Amanda called from Japan to ask if the family wanted to meet her "half way" *in Hawaii*. She had finished her contract and would be going on to work for a Parisian dance company after a short break. Of course we would meet her!

I arranged a reprieve from Stanley and made plans. We found dirt cheap flights using my credit card Air Miles, *(boy, had I earned them!)* and arranged for accommodation at the time share we bought before the market crashed. This was do-able and I was so happy to be able to see my girl again. Brock, Elward, LJ, and his wife all planned to be there, arriving on different flights. I booked mine so I'd be arriving at the airport around the same time as Amanda.

Somehow, in the process of flying cheap, my flight was cancelled. *Your flight has been cancelled.* Not a good thing to hear when your daughter is already on her way to the same destination but flying from the Orient. I had no way to tell her, no way to warn her that she'd be getting off a plane and she would be alone in Hawaii.

I plead my case to the air line and they came through for me. Wow, did they come through for me.

I was in a first class seat, gazing out the window as we descended in a smooth dip over the beautiful Hawaiian Islands. Now, I am arriving earlier than my first planned flight and Amanda and I will have a whole day to ourselves before the rest of the family arrives. It dawned on me that this was just like a moment I had played out in my mind while walking on the promenade, every time I said *"wealth, success"* I had played out a picture like this, flying in comfort, eating only the best food, and now, with my hotel voucher in hand, staying in only the best accommodations. How many times over the last two years had I affirmed wealth and success and equated it to a moment like this? A million? Maybe two? Was this mix up with flights and over-generous airline customer service God's answer to my affirmation? I believe it was—and for the record, it has happened again, since Hawaii. Elward and I have been stranded in some of the most beautiful places on earth, and put up in some of the finest accommodations because it was time for a wonderful mistake like a flight cancellation!

Amanda and I embraced in the airport and went to our lovely hotel. We laughed and she told stories about her stay in Japan, living with three other young women—all of them dancing for Disney. It was an adventure that she would cherish for the rest of her life. We shopped in the cutest shops and wandered the tourist core on our island finding treasures and enjoying every moment of our time together.

The next day, when the rest of the family arrived, it was truly a celebration! We spent eleven days together.

We talked about our favorite literature and LJ introduced me to Florence Scovel Shinn—through a book called, 'The Game of Life.' He had been given a book from a friend and when I opened it up, I said, "This was never meant for you. This book was meant for me!" LJ laughed, but I meant it. I went out to a bookstore and picked up a compilation of Florence Scovel Shinn's writings called, 'The Wisdom of Florence Scovel Shinn, 4 Complete Books.'

With our whole family together, we reset our lives and our goals. We played and ate and laid around hearing stories about world travel and our kid's dreams and plans for the future. And then, all too soon, the future was here and we had to go home, *to Stanley.*

Thank you God for beautiful places, warm waters and clear skies. Thank you for Oprah and Suze, John and Joseph and thank you for my new friend, Florence.

25

We said good-bye to our children and went home, warmed by the memories of long stretches of sandy beach, the sound of the ocean from our hotel window and the laughter of our three children, now grown, but still very connected to one another.

We went home to find Stanley, disturbing as ever—but even a little more troublesome. I tried, I really did, and heaven knows I am not one to give up on anything I have set my mind to. I was going to help this kid and he was going to be well. He was. I used mind power and mantra and prayer and everything I could conjure up to help him. And then, he ran away.

At first it wasn't a big deal, Stanley ran away almost every weekend. But this time, as the days turned into a week and he was nowhere to be found, I got really worried for him. I put all of my energy into it. I kept praying about it, a request for clarity, a request that I'd be able to help Stanley, and if I couldn't, that it would be clear to me and that there would be a safe place for him to reside with someone who could help. I worried and wrote until God sent me an answer—this time, through a dream.

It was not an odd dream to begin with, it started out the way most of my mornings did—with the telephone ringing. I answered the phone and gave support from my bed. Crisis never waits for the dawn. I hung up and got dressed, put on a coffee for Elward, brushed my teeth.

Every methodical normalcy played out in the dream. It was a beautiful day. I slipped on my shoes and kissed Elward and stepped out into the mist. Shuffling down the side walk, I brushed the damp hedges with my fingertips until the street turned and opened up onto the promenade.

"Hello Noelle." It's Stanley, his soft lyrical voice.

I spin on my heel and there he is, stepping out of the bush that I just walked past. He is angelic, his blonde wisps are long, sweeping over his brow and kissing his eyelids, but he doesn't brush them from his eyes. His hands look as though they are tied behind his back. He smiles with his lips, but his eyes are cold.

"Oh, Stanley, where have you been? Don't you know we have been looking for you? Honey we just want to help"—but before I finish my sentence, he hoists an axe from behind his back and plunges it into my skull.

I woke with a gasp and a hand on my head. Thank you God, that was clear enough for me.

26

I quit. I called and told my boss that when they found Stanley, he wasn't allowed back in my home. They found a good place for him with a wonderful, single man who was built big enough to handle an axe wielding child. He would care for him as much as Stanley would allow himself to be cared for.

I learned so much from Stanley about psychosis but even more important, I learned that I wouldn't be able to save everyone.

For now, I'd have to focus on saving Elward. His job was not ideal. All the years of strenuous work and strenuous play had taken their toll. At forty seven years, the aches and pains would prevent him from getting out of bed and going to work in the morning unless he spent 2 hours with his ice packs every night. He was in great shape for his age but too many times the job demanded extreme physical exertion doing the same task for days on end. Competing with twenty and thirty year olds for the position meant out doing them every day, day after day, for as long as he wanted a pay cheque. That meant working through the pain day after day and the ice packs would only make it possible for so long. We wrote together that by the end of the year there would be something different.

God's answer to me came again in the form of a horoscope. He just knew where I'd be looking and when the answer came, I felt it through my whole body.

"To achieve your dreams and goals write them down." I know, I know, there are blurbs like that all over the place, statements like that have almost become cliché. But when I read it that day, in the context of my most fervent prayer for help with our debt load and relationship with Elward's dad, it just filled me with hope. I had done it before, when I was writing lines for John Kehoe. Could I really go back to all that vain repetition when I had come so far in hope and spiritual understanding and prayer?

Just a couple days later, I was standing next to Elward in a book store. He pulled a book right off the shelf and handed it to me like he could read my mind. Henriette Anne Klauser *'Write It Down, Make It Happen.'* I could not believe my eyes. Another answer, another gift. If I wanted this final healing and relief so badly I would have to write it down and make it happen. Henriette's theory is that by writing it down you make yourself believe it is attainable. But there is nothing unspiritual or greedy about her writings. My once vain repetitions on paper now turned into letters to God.

~

Then, the call came to gather in Southern Alberta. The company was growing rapidly and the support centers all across Canada and the USA were not offering the same styles of support. Truehope wanted to coordinate the best support into a call center. They asked me to come out and be the head of that center and Elward to take the position of comptroller.

In all of the hubbub and preparing to move to Alberta, there was never a time that I stopped my affirmations or my prayers. They had become a very serious part of my life. I believed every word I had read in the books of my mentors and although not all of it seemed to apply to me, I took many gifts of knowledge and understanding away from each one of those books. Although I had seen many miracles over the two years of using these new skills, miracles of health, miracles of understanding, financial relief and even luxury. Now it was time to ask for yet another miracle. I began writing a letter to God every day that we would find a home that we could afford, a perfect home, big enough for all. I asked for a newer home with enough bedrooms and bathrooms, and a garage to protect my new car from the weather. I prayed that all our needs would be met and that we would be able to continue to pay off our debt.

Every day at bed time I would write the same thing and I would add a little prayer of gratitude for the day to it. For thirty days I wrote and never missed a day.

Thank you God for Henriette and the inspiration she brought to all of the things I have learned from my mentors. Thank you for Oprah and her inspired ways. Thank you for Suze and her firm lessons. Thank you for John and his basic teachings, thank you for Joseph and his wisdom and spiritualism—the way he gave me what my own father would have if Dad had been living. Thank you for Florence and her insight, and again, thank you for Henriette.

27

We pulled into Lethbridge with a U-haul stuffed to the top with boxes and furniture. We looked for a house for a couple of days and slept at Tony's place and when it became clear that there was no suitable place for us at a price we could afford, we unpacked our truck into Tony's garage and I started writing with more energy than I thought I had. I was affirming that we would have a home—big enough for my kids to visit, with a garage and rooms for hobbies and entertainment. We didn't have a lick of money, so I wrote with a new found determination. We started searching the small towns and local advertisements because homes were so much less expensive in the outlying areas.

After a week of searching, there was nothing and Tony's basement was starting to feel tight. Amanda came home from a contract on a cruise ship with an Australian husband and a baby on the way. They wanted to stay with us until the babe was born rather than go to Australia . . . now we really need a place to live! All four and a half of us packed into Tony's basement and Tony and his wife were accommodating as could be, but in reality, it's not really a smart idea to work with family, and it's even less brilliant to work with them and live with them at the same time! Oh, how we needed a home of our own!

I lay in bed after one very long dinner discussion and told God I needed help right now. I was broke, heavily in debt, tired and homeless—but I was not broken.

Father in Heaven, Infinite Spirit, hear my prayer. I have faith that you will bless me and that my needs and the needs of my family will be met. I know that we are in a mess, but I know that you can heal all things including my financial situation.

I am a good person, I am a loving mother, and I am a very loyal wife. I am worth more than the shacks that people are trying to sell for way too much money. I am worthy of a home with room for my children to come and visit, a garage for our car, (I'll be writing about that one later Lord!), space for hobbies and tools, company and entertaining. I am worthy of a clean space with level floors and a yard with a garden. I am ready for that now Lord. I do not want to live with Tony. I do not want to have our relationship destroyed by familiarity. The eleventh hour has arrived Lord.

The very next day one of Tony's children brought home the local rag from school. This was a small newspaper—legal sized paper folded in half totaling four pages. I had never seen such a small community newspaper! My sister-in-law handed me the paper and said, "There is house for sale in here that you might be interested in."

I looked at it. I could not believe my eyes! A house—just the way I had written it, four bedrooms, only two and a half years old with a double car garage, three bathrooms, and priced at one hundred and twenty thousand dollars. I was stunned.

I called and asked about the house. The man had renters in it so I knew he would understand my plight.

"We have had our house up North put on the market three times in three years and it has not sold. Without selling the house, I don't have any substantial down payment for a purchase. Would you consider a rent-to-own deal so when our home sells we can complete the sale?"

He must have really wanted to sell the house. "Come and see the house and if you like it then we will talk." We were there in a flash!

For the first time, I now had a home that was going to be big enough for all of my kids to visit at once—even with spouses and grandchildren.

"Let's talk about a deal." I said.

"If you secure the house today, I'll lower the house from one hundred and twenty thousand to one hundred and fifteen thousand. I'll let you live here for rent and give you ten months to seal the deal on a mortgage." Was I in a dream or what? Who tells you that they will take $5,000.00 off the price after you decide to buy it? Amanda kicked in with some money and we managed to come up with the five thousand dollar down payment. Just like that, the house was ours. We were able to move in October 15, 2002. We had a home. A real home. The nicest home that we had ever lived in.

I knew I was blessed. That night I wrote an extra prayer, one of my grateful prayers. I wrote clearly and honestly.

Father in Heaven, Infinite Spirit, as I lay in bed in our new home, I come to you with gratitude in my heart. My home is perfect. It is everything I asked for and then some. Father I am grateful for the blessing of this home, the blessings of yesterday, today and tomorrow. There are

so many. I thank you for each and every one of them. I am
truly grateful. I ask that you continue to walk with me and
my family each and everyday.

I was so grateful that I forgot to add the rest. Today,
gratitude was enough.

Now all I need is to sell my other house, qualify for a
mortgage and come up with three hundred thousand
dollars to pay off Elward's dad.

28

Truehope Support kept me very busy. I hired fifty staff from the local community and as they were being trained, I, and a few other seasoned support people scrambled to keep support going for about eight hundred people who were in various stages of recovery from mental illness.

I loved it. I loved the people, the thrill of success, the joy in healing.

The staff started working in full function right at the time the Discovery Health Channel aired a documentary about Truehope. The calls came in and kept coming in. We processed three hundred applications for participation per day and the successes we saw as staff, drew us together as a team. I learned to love the young women who worked for me the same way I loved my dancers. The girls who really took their work seriously stole my heart and I respected them.

We cheered when Laura called in to say she was drug free and better than ever. We laughed when Kevin called in to say that his doctor hardly recognized him and he was ready to go out and get a job. We cried when Tanya said her husband wouldn't support her in using the supplement because it was too expensive. Tanya never had a chance to make us cheer.

Hundreds and hundreds of people came and although some went, many stayed. And I and my staff learned to love every one of them.

One of my favorite parts of managing the support center was the opportunity to give hope to doctors who had reached the end of drug possibilities with hard to treat patients. I spent hours, taking calls from medical practitioners who wanted to support their patient's choice to try the supplement instead of drugs. As I explained the program and the drug reduction methods to the doctors, it thrilled me. Now I was helping people and not just one at a time! Now the doctors would be able to help many people that I would never meet.

~

Fall and winter and spring had passed and now it was time to meet our obligation and secure a mortgage so we could keep our house. All along I had been writing that we would get the funds together or sell our house up North and be able to get a mortgage.

Elward did the math and came up with the amount we needed to sell the house for in order to pay out the second mortgage. Our home, appraised at one hundred and seventy thousand dollars the year we left it would be put on the market once again for only one hundred and thirty-five thousand dollars. At this price, we couldn't afford to list it with an agent. We called and placed the ad on Tuesday and the deal was done by Thursday!

Finally, we'd be free to apply for a mortgage with the hope of continuing to live in our new home.

Our renters were not happy to be leaving the house. They had a terrible tragedy while living there. One of their daughters had a seizure and died in the bath tub and it was a terrible thing for them to have to leave that place. I felt so much compassion for them, but they could not buy the house and after four years, we had to sell it. We just had to. The renters were almost four thousand dollars behind in rent payments and so, out of compassion, Elward and I told them to go on and start fresh, we wouldn't come after them for the past rent. We needed that money, but couldn't bring ourselves to stress them out any more when they had just been given notice to leave the place they called home.

Thank you God, for the blessing of life, and for all of the gifts you have given and will continue to give. Thank you for the immediate sale of our home and I ask that you bless the Smiths that they will find a new place to call home. Thank you for Oprah and Suze, John and Joseph, Florence and Henriette. Thank you for Elward and my three healthy children and thank you for Truehope and my chance to offer hope to people who feel hopeless.

My Turn   106

29

There is no such thing as 'finders keepers, losers weepers' in the universe. If you lose something like we did in lost rental income and lost profit, and you ask for it back, it will come back to you. It is yours to claim.

When we came back to Alberta, we went to get the mortgage for the house. We needed to convince the bank to give us a mortgage for one hundred and ten thousand dollars. We weren't sure we'd qualify given that we still had a lot of debt to pay off and we didn't have any equity in anything. Still, we had to go through the process and hope for the best.

We had the house appraised and the papers came back saying our new house was worth one hundred and forty thousand dollars. We had gained twenty-five thousand dollars in equity before we ever made a payment on the mortgage! Just one more of many miracles manifested right in front of our eyes.

Thank you God for a home that is now my own. You are my immediate source of supply presenting me with all my needs in the right place and at the right time. I am truly grateful.

30

Florence Scovel Shinn taught me that my faith and my intention could be utilized for a person who did not have enough strength of their own. Somewhere in her writings, I read that Florence did treatments for people. It got me thinking. Could I teach my children what I was learning through the gift of a treatment? As it turns out, Brock gave me the perfect opportunity to find out just after we had settled ourselves in our Southern Alberta home.

Brock stayed in Vancouver when we left. He was teaching dance at a couple of studios and wanted to make a life for himself in a city that was full of life and art and entertainment.

Brock fit well into the arts scene in Vancouver. Brock was the life of the party, and living a life of parties. He worked hard and played hard and drinking was a big part of his playing. His partying lifestyle had gotten him fired from a couple of cruise ships. Not that he was dancing drunk, but that he was drinking way too much on the side. Brock took up with a room mate who, for personal reasons, left the apartment and re-rented the room to another far less desirable roommate. Brock was stuck living with a miserable man who was not a friend in any way. This roommate, in the middle of a divorce, filled Brocks home with every form of verbal abuse and miserable behavior. Brock had nowhere to go. He was stuck and to cope with the stress, his drinking escalated beyond partying to making it through the day. Then, we thought our prayers for Brock were answered. He had a sudden break of luck and was able to move out of the apartment to take a room with an old friend. They occupied a room in a mansion in North Vancouver. But, instead of improving, the drinking got worse, and not just drinking, pot smoking too. Then came the dabbling in other drugs. We had only been gone ten months and our son's life was a shave off implosion. It would take a terrible threat, the kind that would cost him his whole future and career to make him want to clean up. The shock he needed came the day his friend revealed how they were paying the rent on such a lavish accommodation. The "off site server room" was not for computers at all. International work is a life line for dancers until they make it in Hollywood. If Brock were even associated with any illicit activity he'd lose his ability to travel, and his whole career with it. He needed out; he needed to get clean right now.

Brock slammed his belongings in storage and called in a favor with a cousin—crashing at his apartment until we could get there.

~

"Hey Mom, Dad." I turn to see Brock against a back ground of busy airport travelers. Then drop my bag and go to hug him. He is skinny, gray, and his eyes are bagging and dull.

"Brock. You look like hell!"

"Aww, that's nice. Thanks Mom." He tries a smile and runs a trembling hand through his strawberry hair, bushing it off his forehead. "C'mon, is it that obvious?"

"Let's get you out of here and get something to eat." I lead him ahead of us, and turn to watch Elward pick up the bags, his gaze meets mine and I know he is every bit as sick as I am for our son who is wasting away.

In the car, Brock is lighthearted, the way he always puts on. "Well, you've got one week to sort me out Mom. I have to be in Edinburgh for the annual International Dance Festival by next Thursday."

"What do you need?"

"A place to live would be good."

"What do you have?"

"I still have my bed and dresser." He smirks in the rear view mirror like it was funny. But that's Brock, an entertainer to the bitter end. "Oh, and this, I still have this baby." He pats the dash of the midnight blue Volkswagen Jetta, "But not for long eh? 'Cause I can't make the payments."

"Two jobs. You are partying away the money from two jobs." Elward speaks in a level calm that I will never master.

"It's not like that Dad. . ." But we all know it is, so Brock won't carry on the excuse.

After an evening with his Dad and me talking straight and stern, it was decided. He turned in his car and the keys. It was the only thing he could do. Problem one solved. But, without the car, he'd have to give up one of the jobs and so his budget suddenly became painfully tight. I cried for him.

"We need to let him go through this Noelle. It's his life and it's his lesson to learn. You have to let him." Elward said as he held me to his chest and let me cry.

"We could fix it now. We could do something for him."

"Let him go through this reality honey, find another way to help him without bailing him out with money."

Elward was right and it got me thinking. As a mother I had a lot more to offer than money. This could be solved in a permanent way if I could just impart some of my faith to Brock.

The budget that we laid out was tight; it was all based on how many hours he would have at the one studio that he still worked for. He seemed relieved when he went off to rehearsal that night. I began to look in the papers for a place for Brock to rent. The prices in Vancouver were insane. He needed a place of his own, one that would let him ground himself—avoiding the all night party scene. And there was only one way I could see this happening.

I wrote for hours, the way Florence taught me. I laid out exactly what Brock needed. I explained that there needed to be an improvement in his life that he was too valuable to lose to the madness of the city. I asked for an apartment, I asked for furniture, I asked for a computer—everything he needed to step out on his own. I explained how he needed a place to live where he would not have the stress of trying to live for others, a place where he could heal. I wrote it all.

The next day, we went out to look at apartments that I had listed for viewing. A few apartments in, it came time to see a loft. I always thought that on an artist level—Brock was a genius, and we soon discovered that the loft in the ARC building was just the place for a creative genius like Brock. To rent here, you needed an artist's portfolio. There were studios everywhere. They had a paint room, a photography black room, a pottery room and kiln, wood work shop, a music studio, and a painting room all at his disposal. Everything Brock had a passion for in his life . . . they had it. He applied for and was accepted to rent a tiny eight hundred square foot loft for eight hundred dollars.

He could take possession next week, before his trip to the festival. Problem two solved.

That afternoon we went to the Brick where Brock applied for a Brick card. When they gave him a two thousand, one hundred dollar credit limit, it was obvious word had not gotten out that he had turned in his car to the dealership. Just another small miracle to be grateful for. And then, yet another small miracle — when they tallied all of the items Brock picked out for his apartment he had spent two thousand, one hundred and twenty dollars. He was twenty dollars over the limit and the store was closing, so the sales manager told him not to worry about it. It was a 'Go, be gone, get out, we want to go home'—type of don't worry about it. In only twenty four hours, Brock had been given every item I wrote for, with the exception of a computer. He needed one desperately if he was to continue his work. He had the computer by the close of business the next day. Everything I asked for, wrote for, everything I prayed for, everything Brock needed, we got. All the needs were met.

Thank you God for every mentor. Thank you for Florence and her teaching me that I can bless my children with my faith.

31

Later, as we prepared his apartment for the furniture Brock realized just what a miracle he was living.

"Mom, how does this work? You have to teach me." Brock asked from his place on the floor. His gaunt face was now better, at least hopeful.

"How does what work?

"The whole write and get it thing.

I want to have this conversation. This is truly an answer to my prayers for Brock. *Please let me teach him what I know. Let me teach him to help himself.*

I lean on the window sill to take a break from the dusting.

"It's what I have been learning about Brock. It's all about recognizing your place in the universe and asking the Infinite to give you what He wants you to have. He wants to grant you everything you need, want and desire, Brock. You deserve happiness, and peace. He wants you to have peace. All you have to do is ask and then be willing to do your part. Set your intention and believe it will be, and the Infinite will direct you to it or bring it to you."

"I can't do it. Mom, I can't think the words and I can hardly write. Just look at me."

I look him over. My scrawny, sickly boy on the floor, with a rag in his hand and sweat on his brow. It has been four days, and he is still shaking like an old man. I can see that he is broken, not just physically, but spiritually too.

Florence Scovel Shinn's words come to me again and I know I can help my boy to help himself, to invite the power of the Infinite into his broken world.

"I'll help you son. Don't worry about it. I'll teach you and you will just get better from here."

I borrowed phrases from Florence and wrote a mantra for Brock and gave it to him before we left..

I do not limit God by seeing limitations in myself. With God, the Infinite Spirit, and myself, all things are possible. I give thanks now for millions which are mine by divine right that now pour in and pile up under grace in a miraculous way. My supply is endless and immediate, all my financial needs are met, and all doors are wide open. I show that I believe, and his promise will be kept. Ask and you shall receive, believing anything is possible. Thank you Lord for my wealth, thank you for my home, thank you for my family, for my parents and for my grand parents who believe in me. Thank you for my friends, thank you for my talents and for the opportunities I can give to others. Thank you for all blessings I receive each and every day. I am truly grateful,
Your loving son, Brock.

He took it and used it like medicine. Writing religiously, pouring over it every night. And like I knew it would, things turned around for Brock almost immediately.

Brock used his new computer to write a dance production for the stage. He presented a teaser of the production at the Vancouver International Dance Festival where he drew the attention of one of the festival producers. Now, he and the producer are seeking funding to produce Brock's first original show. Brock is brilliant, and Brock is steady. He writes every night, invoking the power of the Infinite in his life and asking that all of his needs will be met—and he is never without what he needs. He lives in a bigger loft now, complete with a dance floor for private lessons. He works, teaching at the studio and as a guest teacher for Tap all across North America. Seeing him now, I know that we will never have to revisit that dark day, and I am so grateful for that.

The greatest blessing that will ever be in writing my letters to God is not in the answers that come for my earthly needs, but in the peace that comes in knowing that He is listening and meeting my needs every hour. That is real peace.

Thank You God for Florence Scovel Shinn and for her gifts of wisdom. Thank You for Oprah and Suze Orman and for the last twenty nine pages of her book that gave me hope for a better life. And most of all, thank you for Brock, one of the brightest lights in my life. Life is never boring when Brock's around, and that's a blessing all its own!

32

When news got out in Fort St. John that we had sold the house there for less than it was worth, Elward's dad was furious. *It wouldn't have sold at any other price.* The perception of lost profit brought up all of the old feelings, the whole battle relived once more. Now a good portion of our debt to him was unsecured and he was very unhappy. I watched Elward's heart break all over again.

I decided that I was going to write everyday from October to December for a very large amount of money. I'd be asking for six hundred thousand dollars. I took every debt that we owed, every single penny, including mortgages, loans, credit card debt, cars, everything — and it came to six hundred thousand dollars. I asked God to bless me with this by December eighteenth. *That's only two hundred thousand dollars a month Lord.* Was I out of my mind? I didn't think so at the time. In my prayers I wrote everyday, I claimed that with this money I would rebuild a relationship between a father and a son. That was all that mattered. I just figured if I was going to ask for three hundred thousand for his Dad that I might as well ask for the rest of our debt to be gone all at once. If He could come up with three hundred thousand, then why not six?

And so it went. I wrote every day, and every day I claimed that blessing. I bought lottery tickets and went back to some of my lottery mantras thinking that maybe God would need a hand. Had I learned nothing yet? Since when does the Infinite need a hand? I really believed I was showing courage and faith. *But if all else fails, a lottery ticket might help too.*

I prepared for December eighteenth, believing wholeheartedly that the money was coming. On December fifteenth I wrote a letter to Elward's dad. It was a nice note saying I hoped that the relationship between he and Elward could be rebuilt. I was sorry for the damage that was done when he and I fought. Florence calls this "digging your ditches"; Henriette says "leap and the net will be there." I left the envelope open so I could slip the check in when the money came in the next three days. On December seventeenth, I showed God just how much faith I had and baked beautiful homemade cookies. I wrapped them in tissue and packed them in a tin. I put them in the freezer with a note that these were for Elward's dad when the money came in the next morning. Then, December eighteenth came and December eighteenth went. The money did not manifest itself, and I was so very sad.

I lay in the tub that night and wailed. I howled and sobbed and clenched my fists and shook my head. Had I been overlooked? Had I asked for too much? I got up the next morning and sent the cookies without the letter and without the precious check. *This was not a test God . . . this was the real thing.* How could it be that with infinite power and infinite compassion and infinite resources, He couldn't come up with a measly six hundred thousand dollars when I asked for it?

I had spent two months, filling my days counseling the mentally ill and as many nights counseling God. I knew how it had to happen and I had decided what would be. The problem was I had not yet learned that God does not always do things the way I would have them done. When I realized that I had been a little presumptuous, I got back to writing, this time I'd be simplifying my request.

Dear God,

I know I have assumed a lot and claimed that my way was the only way of doing things, but I can't give up on this. I'm not going to. I am not giving up. I am not giving up on you and I am not giving up on this. I need this problem between my husband and his father to be resolved and I have enough faith that this will happen. It must happen.

I had not conceded that the dead line was wrong. But I stopped writing about getting a specific amount of money. And I stopped buying lottery tickets. Now my emphasis was on getting peace. Peace for Elward, peace for Elward and his dad. And me. Peace for me.

33

It was January the first time Kate called to ask about buying our old dance studio building, I knew Kate and the thought was really very funny. I chuckled. She was running a shrunken down version of my dance studio in the building and she did not have any money. I told her to go ahead and find financing and give me a call. The offer didn't excite me. There was no offer, only an excited young girl dreaming of renovating and expanding and she didn't have the resources to pull it off. I forgot all about it for two months, until she called again.

"Hi Noelle, it's Kate."

"Oh. Hi Kate."

"Yeah, hi, um, I was just calling you again about buying out the dance building?"

"I don't know Kate. Did you figure out how much the renovations were going to cost you?"

"Well sure, I mean I've been working on it. I think I can get some help up here to get things together for financing."

"Do you have money down?"

"No."

"The building is worth a whole lot of money Kate. How are you going to get financing without any money down?"

"Well, I'm working on it."

"Look, let me talk to Elward about it and I'll get back to you."

I didn't talk to Elward and I didn't bother calling her back. Things at work were getting stressful; there were a lot of people coming onto the program and a whole lot of people leaving. The staff was stressed and I was way to busy to play pipe dream games with Kate.

It was April the third time Kate called. I heard her out and got off the phone and laughed. Kate getting financing for that much money would be like the ultimate mind power story . . . she's so determined that that building is hers. *Maybe it's actually possible.* We had the property appraised.

When the appraisal came in, Elward and I spent the evening doing the math. We suddenly realized that after all these years of paying a mortgage and collecting rental payments we had enough equity in that building to pay off all but twenty one thousand dollars of the money we owed Elward's dad!

When we told Kate the price of the building, there was no way she could pull it off.

I made a phone call to Elward's dad and asked him to consider using the equity from the building to pay our debt to him and then refinance for Kate. He jumped at the chance to forgive his son and put the pain behind him. He did the paper work and when all was said and done, we had paid off two hundred and seventy thousand dollars to him and owed only twenty one thousand more. Kate got her building and, more importantly, Elward got his father back.

Was this the answer to all of my writing and prayers? You bet it was! God came up with exactly what it took to relieve the pressure on the relationship between

Elward and his dad, and we were left accountable for our own part of the debt. What a wonderful gift! God gave us what we needed and gave Kate what she needed in the process. I did not get what I was asking for when I named the amount and the date of delivery, but I did get the answer I was truly praying for.

Thank you God for peace in my world. Peace for Elward, peace for his Dad, and peace for me. Oh, thank you!

34

I watched a whole lot of people try the Truehope program. I watched many recover and heal and go on to healthy, normal lives. I watched many more try, get a great reaction at first, and then fall into long term withdrawal from their previous drugs. I watched, over and over, as addiction to psychotropic drugs kept people from getting well. Of course, all of this was before the FDA started warning people about the addictive nature of the anti-depressants and psychotropics. Now they call it 'discontinuation syndrome' the symptoms of which include panic attacks, angina, asthmatic symptoms, headaches, diarrhea, vomiting, and electric shocks in the extremities, insomnia, depression and suicidal thoughts. Back then it was *'My doctor says the drugs are not addictive, so if I'm having weird symptoms it's because I'm mentally ill and need to get back on the drugs—syndrome '*. I couldn't talk to all of them. I couldn't teach all of them what I knew. I couldn't give them the resolve to stay with it, past the withdrawal—to wait it out and find the peace and health that I knew was just around the corner.

I remember one day supporting a mother who was suffering so badly, her heart was broken. Her hyperactive children were now in school and the school was demanding that they get medical attention. The doctor prescribed Ritalin, and when she refused to drug them, the local government came in and removed the kids from her home. I was appalled. It never should have come to this for her. If she had only known how to prevent the illness in the first place she would have two healthy children.

"We are doing this all wrong Elward." Another conversation from the pillow.

"What are we doing wrong?" He turns to look at me.

"The support. We are waiting to tell people how to be healthy when they are already sick. We are no better than the medical system. We are waiting until they have been diagnosed, hit rock bottom, gotten addicted to harsh drugs and have no other place to turn. It's ten times harder to come back from all of that than to do it like Amanda. With her, we caught it before it got started, before she was too far gone. Before she was even really sick."

"Hmmm, do I hear a plan coming or a big train?" he smiles. He knows my thoughts before I even think them.

"I just think that we need to change how we approach this. We need to get to the people before the illness gets to them. That is the only way to stop the madness."

Nothing came of my idea. Perhaps my communication in a board room was lacking. Perhaps the stress of seeing good people fail on a great program was too much for me. Day after long day I sat and watched. I still cheered for the successes, but I was sick for the lost ones; the men and women who came to us because it was their last resort, expecting relief and finding that all of the drugs they had consumed would make their recovery another mountain to climb. I cried a lot. I wrote a lot, I prayed non stop. And, I yelled. I yelled in the board room.

Dear God,

I need to get out of here. I want to offer something more than this. I need to help people to get well before they get sick. They don't need to be insane or stoned or overweight before they look for help. All of these things are preventable. They don't have to learn all of these lessons the hard way like I did. Lord, help me. Let me do my part. Let me be a messenger of Truehope. Show me the way to end the madness.

35

In the fall of 2004, Elward and I were driving in the mountains. It was there that my answer came. I didn't need a horoscope or a book, this one came straight to my mind, and for a moment, my mind and heart connected in a most powerful way. Like a whisper to my soul came the words, 'It's time to write a book, and start sharing what you know.'

"Elward."

"MmmmHmm."

"Do you remember when I first started doing mind power—that horoscope that I read standing in line at a coffee shop early one Saturday morning?"

"Which one?"

"The one that said 'You will share your new discovery with many people, friends and family and those you've yet to know'."

"I remember."

"Well the time has come. I just all of a sudden . . . I feel very inspired to write a book."

Elward thought it was a good idea. So, I tried.

My niece had just finished writing her own book and she agreed to help me with mine. She gave me a long list of writing assignments that would help me get to the core of the story, and do a whole lot of healing in the process. I took the list and that was as far as I got with the project. I just couldn't get my writing to flow. I wasn't ready.

Meanwhile, things at the office got worse and worse for me. My heart was no longer in the work I was doing, and I did not feel like I was supported when I wanted to do things differently. It's the frustration of working in a place that you don't belong, when your heart and mind are elsewhere and your mission is going unfulfilled. Every day was gray, every night was frustration. It wasn't that the work wasn't good or worthy of my effort; the people needed to be helped, but I felt my role was going by the wayside to satisfy the company's need to stay the course. There was no room for creativity in our approach. There seemed to be no way to satisfy both the company needs and my own, so I'd have to create one.

I went to the company with a proposal to get me out of the office. They agreed to send me to the States as a sales representative for general health promotion to chiropractors. I set up my office and waited for the resources that the company was to send me. Nothing came. I did what I could, and nothing came of the effort. So, in my solace, I started writing. With writing came new perspective, and healing. All in all, I spent four months writing and healing before the company called me back to Canada.

When I came back, my position in the company was filled, my desk was gone and I was totally displaced. I couldn't find my place in anything anymore, but the feeling didn't last. Tessa, who was now working for Truehope in Norway had come back to Canada for a visit, and she brought with her another message from God.

We are driving in my car and I am telling her about all of my frustrations and how nothing I am doing is moving forward. It has shaken my confidence, my belief that I ever had a role in helping other people come to full health. Her answer is so simple, "Have you heard of Wayne Dyer?"

"No."

"He was on television last night on PBS and it is showing again tonight. You really need to hear what he has to say."

I taped the special and watched it over and over again. Then I got his book. Wayne finished my healing with one simple statement.

'When you change the way you look at things, the things you look at change.'

I had new hope. Hope that I could change the direction I was going simply by seeing things differently. The desires of my heart needed to be the direction of my mind. With Wayne, I would learn how to put my mind where my heart was.

Thank you, God, for the inspiration and gifts that come when I am ready to receive them. Thank you for Oprah, Suze, John and Joseph. Thank you for Florence and Henriette, and thanks so much for Wayne.

36

Elward and I were so happy to be reunited. We had been separated for the four months that I was gone, and it was one of the hardest times of my life—to be so far away from him. He had stayed to continue his work as the comptroller for the company, but he was unhappy without me.

The time I spent away was used not only for writing, but for reflection. I wanted so badly for Elward and me to be able to work as a team. It was something I wrote for daily. I wasn't even home yet when the company called him in and offered him a new position with me in company promotions. What a gift! All things were coming around again. Even the things that I didn't know I wanted back.

One morning, as I was checking our bank accounts on the computer, a familiar old scene replayed. "Elward, you'd better come and take a look at this."

It was stock once again, dead, old, Science and Tech. The remnants that were inadvertently left over keeping an account open when we had lost all hope of ever seeing it come back. I would trade again, but this time with a different perspective and a constant remembrance that the Infinite is the giver of all good gifts and that this money and the success to come would be exactly that, a gift from God.

Everything was coming around in full circle. All things that had once been taken from me were given back again. My writing began to flow and my book started coming together; and soon, our dream of doing health seminars started to come together as well.

There was no velvet curtain the first time I stepped on stage for my new role in Truehope; just a three inch platform, an overhead machine and seventeen senior citizens in the audience. *Finally Lord, this was the real thing.* I talked about disease prevention, the resolution of mental illness, the healing of brain injury using nutrition. I shared new advances in science and stories of the people I had served while I worked in Truehope Support. I watched the nods and the smiles and the understanding in my small audience.

I spoke from the heart and the high I felt from sharing my new world with those people was every bit the high I had felt the day I accepted the accolades, roses and applause in my old life.

I came home and wrote again.

My path is straight, my conviction sure, and I know that there is healing to be found, even before the hurt, when we have a healthy mind, a healthy body, and a healthy heart, we will be free before we are ever in bondage. Just put your mind where your heart is.

Thank you God, for Elward, my eternal support, and for my three healthy children LJ, Brock and Amanda. Thank you for my good daughter-in-law and my faithful son-in-law. Thank you for my two beautiful grand children and the joy they bring to my world. Thank you for the peace that has allowed my grandchildren to meet their great grandfather. Thank you for Oprah and Suze, John and Joseph, Florence and Henriette, and Wayne. Thank you for clarity of thought and energy to take action. Thank you for the gifts that you give, of life and wealth and freedom, for all of the blessings of yesterday, today and tomorrow, given by the power of your Infinite Spirit. Thank you. Today, I ask for nothing Lord, for all of my needs are truly met.

Your Turn

Tapping in

to the untapped power of the other mind

There is a power all around us that most of us know nothing about much less that it is available for our use at any time. All of our universe consists of the same components; minerals, vitamins, electrons, neutrons, protons. These elements all exist in such a fashion that they have a vibrational frequency that is measurable with instruments that modern day science has made available. This frequency ranges from the very low range of rocks to the very high range of thoughts, but one thing is true for all: interaction with another object with a different frequency will alter the frequency of both. This is how water will make a rock smooth, wind will create pillars of stone in the desert, and a woman or man will attract a mate. Is it then such a stretch of the imagination to assume that a thought will attract like energies from the entire universe, a universe composed of nothing but energy? While this may seem like a giant leap of faith, these concepts have been addressed in many different ways in the past. The contention that our subconscious mind is somehow connected to a greatness beyond our comprehension is not new. Modern religion has adopted the acceptance of the Holy Ghost and that its inclusion in our bodies grants to us the ability to ascertain good from evil and to access to some extent the power of God that is available to us through this gift. The Eastern religions tend to imply access to these gifts and powers by purging ourselves of vain and selfish thoughts and working toward attaining enlightenment and thereby accessing the powers of the universe. In all forms of advancement there is one common theme; that of the advancement of unselfish and selfless pursuit of good, the love of others above the love of one's self. This common theme is also the root of accessing the power inherent in yourself.

From ancient days, writings have admonished things such as "For as a man thinketh in his heart, so is he." (Proverbs 23:7). Why is this? Because whatever energy your thoughts are broadcasting is the energy that is rushing back in response to that broadcast. Whatever you think for yourself becomes your reality. Whatever you wish for others also becomes your reality because of the attraction of the universal energy. Your thought patterns, those predominant in your conscious mind are scored into the malleable matter of your subconscious mind. Your subconscious mind is your connection to the power and intelligence of the universe. Whatever you tell it, it works overtime to make happen. If the only messages that it is getting are doom and gloom what do you think it is looking for and attracting for you? Wouldn't you rather it was looking for your success, health and wealth? So if it is that easy why isn't every one healthy, wealthy and successful? In Harrison B.C., every fall teams of enterprising people gather to build the most impressive sand sculptures. In just a few hours one person could absolutely demolish the work done by a whole team over several days. Would it be reasonable to expect one person to rebuild this magnificent sculpture in just a few hours? Of course not. What takes hundreds of man hours to build can be torn down in just a few man hours but can only be rebuilt by hundreds of man hours of labour. In spite of this we expect that we can tear down 20 or 30 or 40 years of self-defeating thoughts and totally rebuild them and change our lives and our circumstances and our futures in just a few days. If we could only convince ourselves that it is reasonable to expect that it will take months or even years to change the habits of decades then we would have the patience to persevere until we see the results. What we must decide first and foremost is to choose the road that we will travel, because that road will lead to the success that we want for ourselves. Then, as Henriette Klauser says in 'Write it Down, Make it Happen' "If you are headed in the right direction, all you need to do is keep walking".

Napoleon Hill in his book tells the tale of a gold miner who mined his claim until it ran out of gold and eventually sold it. The new owners renewed the assault on the mountain and within three feet of where the previous owner had given up found a new and rich vein of gold. "One of the most common causes of failure is the habit of quitting when one is overtaken by temporary defeat". – Napoleon Hill. You are never defeated until you admit defeat for as long as you continue to play you are still in the game. Were we as dogged in our pursuit of excellence as we are in our acceptance of defeat our world would be a totally different place.

Our natural existence is one of harmony. All the different parts of our body are designed to exist in harmony and to work together for the efficient existence of the whole. The world around us has been designed in the same fashion. Each plant works in harmony with all other plants and provides shelter for some animals, food for others. This allows them to perform their designed function, which may be to provide food for other animals. If an outside force destroys a piece of this harmonious system, the entire system is thrown out of balance. If the item destroyed is the food source of a species then that species is threatened. If that species is the food source for another species then that species existence is threatened, and so on and so forth. In the same way, the entire universe has its own balance and harmony. The scale upon which this balance is weighed exceeds our comprehension but we can still use the elementary principles we can understand to our benefit.

When we tamper with the harmony of the universal energy by informing our subconscious mind in no uncertain terms that which it knows to be false, it introduces a disharmony that must be corrected. For example, you weigh 160 pounds and you wish to be 115 pounds. When you do your affirmation and repeat for 10 minutes that you weigh 115 pounds your subconscious knows that this is not true. You have introduced an discontinuity that must be reconciled, and so, in order to restore harmony your subconscious mind will access the universal power and change whatever it has to in order to restore the perfect harmony that it requires.

This makes it easy to understand why we must have absolute faith that what we are asking for will be manifested. This establishes the imbalance that prompts the intercession of the power of the universe. If you don't really believe what you are asking, then your doubt is presenting to your subconscious as strong a message as your request and, therefore, no imbalance is created and no adjustment is necessary to restore harmony.

Thoughts

The conversion from a self-defeating daily routine to a harmonic and success oriented routine can only begin in one place. Whatever you impress upon your subconscious mind through repetition of thoughts will direct your actions and determine what you experience every day. Many people from many different frames of reference have coined phrases that ultimately have the same meaning, e.g. 'you are what you think', 'your words are your destiny', 'you are controlled by your thoughts', etc., etc., etc. Florence Scovel Shinn exemplified the epitome of this concept with her book title 'Your Words are Your Wand.' The inference in this is the goal of retraining your minds; that conscious awareness of the truth of the notion that if you can think it you can have it. Your subconscious mind is a good soldier, it neither argues nor thinks. It just accedes to your request and finds a way to make it happen. Thus, if you wish to have a happy, successful and prosperous life you must regulate your thoughts so that these are the only thoughts your mind is feeding your subconscious.

Many times in my life I had been subjected to self improvement courses, books and lectures that strongly suggested that 'stinkin' thinkin'' was the first obstacle to be overcome in order to begin the path to success. It was not until I was introduced to the concept yet again in my studies on mind power that I became acutely aware of just how much negative thought actually went on constantly in my mind. When you begin to listen to what is actually going on in your mind, you too will realize why you are not obtaining your goals. For me it became a household game because either my daughter or husband always seemed to overhear whenever I said something I should not have. To realize that you are accountable not only for your actions and words but also your thoughts brings a whole new perspective to life. To utilize the tools of your mind to alter those old habits, to stop the negative thoughts, and to speak only positives, is to take control of your future.

One of the worst habits I had to break was the one person argument. Now I realize there is a place for practice and preparedness but that is totally different than engaging in an internal heated argument that encompasses both sides of an issue and all possible points of objection culminating in a negative emotional turmoil. The hormones released by this type of emotional response take 8 – 12 hours to dissipate so when your spouse comes home from work, you have very little control over your greeting. That this has absolutely nothing to do with your spouse is meaningless because you are lost in the hormones and emotions of your solitary dispute. Throughout my professional career (all of them) I have been involved with many people, and the opportunities for these situations has been endless. The discipline to control your mind and your thoughts can release you from the pitfall of this sordid scenario.

How do you begin this daunting task? Every morning when you wake up say to yourself 'I greet this day with a song in my heart, a song of joy, a song of peace, a song of love, and a song of prosperity. I am grateful for this day and all the blessings within it.' Establish the beginning of your day as one of harmony and success.

The next step is to monitor your thoughts and any time you catch a negative thought creeping in, just stop it dead in its tracks. If it happens to be in a conversation either remove yourself from the conversation by saying "I cannot continue this conversation", or change the topic to one you can participate in. Please note that this type of unsavory conversation includes gossip. If it happens to be just in your thoughts, toss that thought out of your head as soon as you recognize it. This can be done by removing it with a concentrated thought, such as, "There is no room for thoughts like this in my life, move them out". This is the method recommended by Joseph Murphy, and the one I found worked for me.

After my disastrous experience with the Stock Markets I was deluged by negative and self defeating thoughts constantly. The loss and the failure had brought lack and doubt, and I was dragged down by it. For weeks it was almost a full time job just casting these thoughts out. I have practiced this for so long that now when I venture into a conversation or thought process where I do not belong, I get the sickest feeling in my gut and an invisible slap on the back of the head that says "WHAT THE HELL ARE YOU THINKING (or saying, or doing)!" I remove myself from the conversation, thought, or situation as quickly as I can.

An alternate method of thought retraining is to catch negative thoughts and transform them into a positive. If you find you are thinking of a lack of money, or the ill effects of being a little short of funds, then think 'All my needs are met and I am thankful for my wealth. I prosper in everything I do'. If you are thinking negatively about someone, then say to yourself as Joseph Murphy recommends in 'The Power of Your Subconscious Mind' "I sincerely wish him (her) well", or, "I refuse to give power to any person, place, or thing to annoy me or disturb me". If you are concerned about competition preventing your success then try "This is a rich universe and there's plenty for all of us."

At first it will not be easy, and the frequency of the thoughts you must banish and transform may be a daunting task. As you utilize the methods I would like to teach you, it will become easier and easier and you will see your life beginning to change. Your life will have no choice but to change because as Wayne Dyer states; "When you change the way you look at things, the things you look at will change." When you realize that everything you desire in life is available to you as you change your mental images to ownership and acceptance of those things, all of these techniques will become second nature to you, and therefore effortless. I have now come to a point where it makes me feel guilty and uncomfortable when I catch myself wandering into areas of thought or conversations that I know are not conducive to my continued success.

Just like a magic wand, your thoughts galvanize your subconscious to tap into the power of the universe and provide you with whatever it is you have asked for. You must be conscious at all times that this universal law is true and you are using it all day, every day, for good or bad.

Fearful thoughts and words create fear
Angry thoughts and words create anger and aggression
Doubtfulness creates doubt and low self-esteem
Thoughts and words of lack create lack

But as with the negative, the same can be said for positive thoughts and words

Words   and   thoughts   of   hope   and   faith   create
manifestations of positive things
Words and thoughts of kindness and love create just that,
kindness and love and harmony
Words and thoughts of abundance and success can create
whatever your heart desires.

Faith

When I went to the John Kehoe course I was not sure what made me think I should go there. I knew nothing of mind power or its' workings, but I did know that Suze Orman told me that things could change if I let them, and I believed her. Perhaps it was that belief that led me to John Kehoe. I remember sitting in the Hyatt on that night in October and never doubting a word Kehoe said. I understood that I needed the knowledge that he was offering to help me get my life back on track, and I believed that if I took his course I would be successful. Was it naivety or faith? I am not sure if even I could answer that question, but I did the exercises as if my life depended on it. As I practiced and repeated and repeated and repeated, my life changed, my outlook changed, and I began to see results and answers appear.

The days and weeks and months went by and my life started to settle into a new pattern, and over and over again the things I asked for were manifested. I think it was because I believed what Suze and John had said. Both of them said that these techniques worked for them, and they would work for anyone who used them. I used their techniques and had faith that I would receive what I asked for.

When I found the writings of Joseph Murphy and Florence Shinn, I discovered that they were firm believers in the role of faith in realizing your desires. I was pleasantly surprised to find that this concept goes all the way back to the Bible. "Whatsoever ye shall ask in prayer, believing, ye shall receive." Matthew 21:22. "What things soever ye desire, when ye pray believe that ye receive them, and ye shall have them." Matthew 11:24. "If thou canst believe, all things are possible to him that believeth." Mark 9:23. I am not one of those gullible people who believe everything they are told, but I am grateful that I believed this concept without question.

The dictionary defines faith as believing. I accepted this without reservation and wrote, and spoke, and repeated, with firm conviction and faith that what I asked for I would receive. As a result, everything I asked for was manifested to me. As you recall from having followed along in the earlier chapters, the only thing I asked for and have not yet received was the 649 winning.

I give thanks everyday for faith and courage; courage to ask for the things I need, want and desire, and the faith to know that as I ask so shall I receive.

John Kehoe says that you don't even have to believe that what you are affirming is possible, you just have to affirm. In the process of affirming and using affirmations to change your negative thoughts to positive, your low expectations to higher expectations, your attitude toward others to one of benevolence, your failures to successes, will you not also change your belief in the process? Simply by beginning the process you have told yourself that, believe it or not, you have faith that the process will yield to you the outcome you desire.

If you believe and or have faith that this book will change your life as you apply what you have learned from it, then you too will be a part of the faith that I have used in sharing what has helped me, in an effort to enable others to help themselves find a better future. I am happy for you as your life, and the lives of those you touch, is about to change, and grateful that I have been allowed to contribute to that.

Fear

The single most likely element that can stop you on your road to success is fear. It has been said that fear is the mind killer, and upon analysis, that is exactly what it does. Fear stops the reasoning process; it prevents you from beginning because of some intangible reason that you may not even be aware of. The fact that there is nothing to fear but fear itself does not seem to sink in; your first thought instead of your road to success, is one of fear. We live in a world of opposites and for us, this apprehension of disaster, this incessant anxiety, is essentially the opposite of hope. Tapping into the power of your mind is all about hope, there is no room for fear. The thoughts you allow in your conscious mind are conveyed to your subconscious mind, and it acts upon them in exactly the form you have sent them. If your first thought is success and your second thought is fear you will not attract firstly success and then fear, the fear will consume your desire and kill your dreams.

As I mentioned earlier, I lived for a while in fear. I panicked all day long. I cried, wailed, begged and then begged some more. I could not seem to break the cycle that the powerful negative emotions had trapped me in. From the fear came despair so deep that it was closing over my head and there was nothing I could seem to do about it. It took an outside force to intervene and help to restore my balance and harmony. This force for me was my husband; he put half a dozen capsules in my hand and told me to take them. The Truehope multivitamin among other things assists the body by supplying the raw materials it needs to cope with various internal stresses, a replacement for the fuel burned by the extreme emotions. Within three days my despair was lifting and allowing the return of my mind, my heart, and my soul. When I had regained enough control of my thoughts to be able to resume the affirmations that I had learned previously to banish fear and self doubt, I became like David slaying Goliath. Every time the Goliath of a doubt or negative thought or emotion appeared I would immediately attack that thought and move it out, concentrating instead on the manifestation of the things I needed, wanted and desired.

Joseph Murphy said; "Man is born with only two fears, the fear of falling and the fear of noise. All other fears were given to you ... by those who influenced your early years." Shakti Gawain states; "Once we are willing to look fully and deeply at the source of a fear, it loses its power." Shakti continues with the idea that is most important to us; "In your fear of not getting what you want, you may actually be energizing the idea of not getting it as much or more than you are energizing the goal itself." This further emphasizes why we do not have room for fear.

More than anything else the fear itself could prevent the successful attraction of our dreams and desires. The solution is not simple but it is not difficult either. First, identify the source of the fear. Examine it carefully and compare it to what it is preventing you from attaining. Are you quite certain that you want to allow that particular fear to prevent you from getting what you are asking for? Secondly, use the emotions that the arrival of your dreams and desires will bring you to replace any fears when they try to creep in. Focus your thoughts on the manifestations you have already seen as a result of your use of the power of your mind. Concentrate and give thanks for your successes and always remember; if you are on the right path then all you have to do is keep on walking.

Affirmations

Affirmation: to affirm, to assert positively, to confirm. A short and to the point statement of what it is that you need, want, or desire. This short statement must be done in a positive, present-tense manner. There is no room for indecision in an affirmation. You must believe that the desires you are asking for are good for you, will do no harm to another, and will effect a positive change for everyone. You must occupy the position that your desires are yours to have and they exist in your now. In this way you leave no doubt in your subconscious mind about what it is you are asking for. "I need to lose weight" is not an acceptable affirmation. This is aimed tentatively at some time in the future. Decide what you want, set a firm goal, and state it as fact. 'I weigh 125 pounds.' There, now the power of your subconscious mind can go to work making this a reality.

Affirmations can be done out loud or silently to yourself. When I first began affirmations I found my mind was so untrained and unruly that any little distraction would derail my affirmation. I borrowed my husbands' construction hearing protectors, the kind that look like headphones (only not so pretty), so I could eliminate outside noise, and thus limit the distractions to those in my own mind. I removed myself to a quiet area where there were no visual distractions and focused my entire concentration on keeping my mind on my affirmation. Once I managed to train my mind to focus and maintain

---

that focus I was able to do affirmations while driving, standing in line at the bank, even walking around behind my grocery cart.

Affirmations can also be accompanied by visualizations. This adds tremendous power to the affirmation. To see vividly the successful attainment of the affirmation, to enjoy all the benefits, the emotion, the satisfaction indelibly writes the request on your subconscious mind. The immersion in a visualization along with your affirmation can only be used when you can focus your whole attention on the affirmation. Driving is not a good time to try visualization. When you sequester yourself to do your affirmations, visualization will increase the effect immensely.

Establishing the wording of your affirmation may take some time and effort. As the definition states, shorter is better. Don't use ten words where three will do the same job. It is the effect that you are interested in. When you wish to influence your weight you could say something like 'These extra pounds are killing me. Why should I go to dinner when I look so fat in this dress. My kids are embarrassed to tell their friends that I am their mom.' While these may all be true you need to set your goal and that is your affirmation. If your goal is 125 pounds then your mantra could be 'I weigh 125 pounds,' but just as effective would be your visualization combined with '125 pounds.' Your mind is plumb full of all the reasons and all of the connotations of your weighing 125 pounds. Every time you say '125 pounds', these reasons and connotations run rampant in your thoughts and are conveyed to your subconscious mind. To say anything else at all is simply redundant. Revel in the economy of simple direction and enjoy the anticipation of results.

Many who have gone before have suggested that 10 minutes per day for each affirmation is a reasonable compromise between convincing your subconscious mind and being ineffective. I have adopted this as my norm and currently spend 10 minutes each on four different affirmations that I am working on, in addition to my mantra and my meditation. More about these later.

How do you find the time, you ask? That is so simple when you analyze it with your goals and dreams in mind. I give up enough TV time to make sure that I get my affirmations and mantras in every day. I have yet to enjoy a TV show that I can absolutely affirm has changed my life in the way that my affirmations can. (Except maybe for the Wayne Dyer special on PBS), but that is not the TV I am referring to. According to Wayne Dyer our children by the time they reach 14 years of age have witnessed 12,000 simulated murders on TV. When you compare the violence, destruction, mayhem, and the negative connotations of prime-time TV to the positives you want for your life, is there really any question as to the answer? I have taken to writing my affirmations to further reinforce the effect. For each affirmation I spend 10 minutes writing the simple 1, 2, or 3 word affirmation. As I have said previously, your mind can not help but feed the subconscious extra images when you think of a single word or phrase so when you say WEALTH there are images surrounding this concept that are transferred, when you say SUCCESS there are images surrounding this concept that are transferred, when you say CONFIDENCE there are images surrounding this concept that are transferred, when you say HEALTH there are images surrounding this concept that are transferred, when you say 125 POUNDS there are images surrounding this concept that are transferred, and so on.

The most important aspect of all of this is to decide what you want and start to say it as an affirmation. Don't worry if it is not perfect on the first instance; you can fine tune it and polish it as you go along. The important thing is to begin to convince your minds that you want this, you deserve this, and you intend to have this. When you believe and you ask, then it is yours.

Mantras and Prayers

Mantra by definition is a prayer or recitation often used with a meditation exercise. I do not really think of my mantra as a prayer, but rather as a recitation. Mantras are similar to affirmations in that you repeat the same verses day after day, but they are lengthier with more detail. To get the most effect from a mantra it should be recited when you can achieve a relaxed state, such as first thing upon waking in the morning and the last thing before falling asleep at night. At these times the distractions are reduced and the mind can dwell upon the message in the mantra. Those who already have well developed meditation skills can utilize them to do their mantra at any time of the day when they have the solitude required for meditation.

I am a beginner in the art of meditation, as I have throughout my life, had the ability to close my eyes, exhale, and be fast asleep. The meditative state for me therefore requires an extreme amount of concentration to stay awake. I am working on this technique and will be able to offer more substantive recommendations in my next book. I do firmly believe that there is a significant extra benefit to reciting your mantra out loud as discussed in the chapter on writing. Ensure that you are in a place and time that you will not have any impediment to speaking your mantra out loud as any inhibitions will affect the sincerity and dedication of your words and thoughts. I sometimes use my time in the bathtub or the shower for doing my mantras.

Music is a great way to initiate the vibrational energy that is conducive to meditation and mantras. Henriette Klauser recommends doing writing near running water as the energy is particularly conducive to creative thought. I live far from the water so I use some tranquil music that I find aids in achieving the calm state I find effective for my mantra. I sometimes move above the calm and serene and invoke more emotion delivering the mantra as if I were reciting a monologue from the stage. This helps to add the energy of emotion to the message and enhances the vibration that we are sending out to attract to us that same energy.

I also have a few prayers that I use —especially when I am driving. They are different from my mantras and I use them primarily to remind myself of who and what I am, and my relationship to the Infinite, and its' power and knowledge. These are explored in more detail in my lectures.

Disappointments

The most difficult aspect of this new way of dealing with life is the realization that you did not receive what you asked for. As I found out, and you have read previously, this is often because we are looking for what we expected as an answer. The trap is that we often decide how our request should be satisfied, and in so doing, can limit the manifestation, or simply not recognize the answer when it arrives. If you believe that you can ask an infinite power to supply your desire, isn't it a bit redundant to try to tell it how to provide the answer to your request? Allow the power you are accessing to provide you the answer in its own way and you will find that everything works out so much better than you could have planned. After all, do you really think that your mind works better than the universal intelligence you are petitioning?

I employed everything that I had learned about asking and receiving. I utilized affirmations, mantras, visualization and repeated them diligently every day. I set a deadline, determined what charities I would support, how much tithe I would pay, and gave thanks every day, several times a day. When the deadline passed and the 600,000 dollars did not arrive I was devastated, but I did not give up. As a matter of fact the statement that I was not giving up became part of my daily routine. The solution presented itself three weeks later but, as it was not the answer that I had determined I would receive, I did not recognize it and actually did not recognize it for three more months.

Sometimes the things we ask for can not be provided in the time frame that we have requested. Some of our requests may necessitate that events elsewhere be completed before ours can be addressed. If your requests are slow to arrive, perhaps you need to do a reality check. Is what you are asking for really in your best interest? Does it carry with it the potential to harm anyone? Is it really good for all the people involved? Do you sincerely and fervently believe that it will manifest itself for you? If you are absolutely certain of the answers to all these questions, then persevere and watch for the answer. It may not be in the form that you anticipated. You may be ignoring the answer because you have not allowed yourself to recognize it.

Like any other learned skill this takes time and patience and practice, and will get better the longer and more ardently you practice it. The more you practice, the easier it will be. The results will be evidenced faster and more frequently, and the more likely you will be to recognize them. Crucial to this is the profound realization that if you ask for nothing that is exactly what you will get, over and over again. Do not make the mistake of giving up, for you never know when the answer is just one more request away. Ask that your mind and your heart be open to receive the answer, for when it arrives it may be so much better and bigger than you anticipated, that you will have no chance of recognizing it without expanding your perceptions.

Gratitude

The one thing that I would like to have every reader of this book take with them and keep with them as a daily habit would be the expression of gratitude. The transition to a positive and expectant attitude largely depends on the recognition of the good in your self, your life and the people around you. It is the small things we take for granted that give everyone a base for giving thanks. Give thanks for your health. Give thanks for the dirty dishes because it means you have eaten. Give thanks for your bills because they mean you have heat, lights, water, a roof over your head, a bed to sleep in. Give thanks for the sun that lights your way in the daytime, the moon that lights the night, and the stars that decorate the night sky. Give thanks for the birds that sing such a happy song as they give thanks for a crumb or a seed. Give thanks for your healthy children, or the healthy children you will have. Give thanks for your boss, for without him you may be unemployed.

As you learn to give thanks and be grateful for whatever it is that you have, you open the doors to attract more of those positives into your life. As you begin to see the manifestations of your requests, always give thanks for those answers, and never stop giving thanks for those answers, for to stop is to forget. Once you begin to forget how blessed you are, discouragement begins to replace your peace and harmony, and the good you wish for yourself will be replaced by whatever your thoughts are attracting.

I have developed a habit of giving thanks all day long as I find small answers to small expectations. I give thanks for a sale in the grocery store, a markdown sticker on the piece of meat I want, the parking spot that opens up as I drive up to the front of the store, the fact that I dropped my keys in the snow . . . just as the wind blew the locked car door closed. I end each affirmation session with a thank you for the receipt of whatever it is that I have asked for.

Once each week I put a nice piece of meditation music on and sit in a comfortable spot and write all the things I am grateful for. Writing pages and pages of all the things for which you are thankful is a wonderful way of reinforcing in your mind, and your thoughts, just how far from bad things really are, and it helps to give more hope for the future.

Try giving thanks in writing. Do not begrudge any little thing without considering what your life would be without it. I am sure you will find this a very rewarding exercise, as I have. As you train your mind to ask for and expect nothing but the best, and give thanks for each baby step, always expressing your gratitude for all the blessings of yesterday, today and tomorrow, you will not be disappointed.

Visualization

For some people, my self included, the concept of visualization is daunting if not impossible. In my quest for a better life and the teachings of others that this journey took me to, visualization was noted as an instrumental aspect of those who are truly successful. I worked hard on all the things I read and learned in an effort to satisfy my desire for the things I dreamed of. The more I worked on it, the easier it became, but no one put it in simpler terms than Wayne Dyer when he phrased it "Thinking from the end." When you think of it in those terms all of a sudden it is totally different.

When I was young I used to think about the time when I would grow up and get married and have children. I am sure we all thought these things when we were young and were establishing our aspirations and trying to decide what we would be when we grew up. I remember the picture I had in my mind of me in my white bridal gown on my wedding day and everything was so beautiful and perfect. As children, our use of imagination is natural, expected, and our use of it is in living colour. This is visualization at its peak—allowing our imagination to play for us the video clip in colour of our goal come to fruition.

In my life as a dance instructor I would encourage my students to play the music for their performance and go through the entire routine in their mind; every step, every movement, every expression. This technique could be used to practice and imprint the details of the routine in their minds in any place, at any time, so that they would not forget it when they were on stage in front of the audience with the lights in their eyes. At the time I had no idea that I was suggesting they use visualization techniques, and perhaps it was better that I did not know the technical term at that time.

I was introduced to the technique at a Hospital Board Convention I had attended while serving as a board member. Peter Jensen author of *"The Inside Edge"* had been a guest speaker and had shared how he works with athletes to develop the mental skills that allow them to excel in their field. I figured if it worked for them it could work for my dancers. The realization that I understood the concept even though I did not know the name, made visualization seem ridiculously easy. All I had to do was to imagine what I wanted.

As a young dancer myself, I had a poster with the caption "If you can see it and believe it you can achieve it." This phrase welds the different disciplines together into a very powerful whole. Visualization, when used in conjunction with affirmations or mantras, super charges the message. To begin with, you may want to find a quiet place and use meditation to quiet and calm your brain and let your mind drift easily into the realm of imagination and fantasy. Build pictures of the goal you seek while you express the thoughts, repeating the request, statement, or outcome. As you develop the pictures of what your success looks like, you will reach the point of beginning your affirmation and pressing play on your internal DVD player. Enjoy the movie as it shows you the result you desire. For each of your goals you will have a specific set of pictures, or video clips, to reinforce and bolster the verbal request.

The concept of visualization is not mine but I do hope I have managed to propose it in terms that you are able to understand and utilize in your own life. The emotional impact of seeing your success will empower your requests and entrench in your subconscious mind the scenario it needs to present to you.

Intuition

There are many different ways people explain how they are influenced to make a decision. Some call it a hunch, for some it is a small voice within, or an invisible tap on the shoulder, a thought that appears seemingly out of nowhere. Some refer to it as the promptings of the spirit within them that helps and guides them. No matter what you would like to name this power we have, it still works the same way. Like any other talent it can be strengthened by use; perfected by listening to its' promptings.

One of the most important sayings I learned in my studies was quite simply that the infinite power that surrounds us all is my immediate source of supply. One of the aspects that I enjoy, now that I have begun to hone the ability of this immediate source, is that when I need help with a decision I can depend on the infinite power and knowledge of the universe to present to me the answer. As I state this in my mantra every day, and have for many years, I now expect and look forward to the promptings of that still small voice within, or if I am not paying attention it comes as a slap in the back of the head (not a painful one, but insistent).

When is a thought just a thought? How do you decide if a thought is a prompting of your intuition, or just a random thought? When you are affirming that you are in tune with your connection to the power of the infinite—and that it is your immediate source of supply, then failing to respond or act upon the answers it sends to you weakens the connection. The more you listen, the more finely tuned your intuition becomes, and the answers will come easier, faster and more frequently. I was watching a talk show on TV one day and the woman being interviewed, an expert on intuition, told her story of receiving a strong intuition not to get on her flight. The message was so strong and so powerful that she listened and was on the ground when the flight she was to be on flew into the World Trade Center building. We have all heard similar stories before and have asked ourselves how this could possibly work. Well, the answer is simply to learn to develop the talent by tapping into the power within us and strengthening it through every day use until it becomes our constant advisor.

I now get answers, direction or ideas at any time of the day or night; while driving, sleeping, showering or walking on my treadmill. The more I listen to them, the more I can count on them to be there when I need them. Some of the greatest people in history have attributed their success to their hunches, gut feelings, or ideas that seem to materialize out of thin air. Being in tune and in harmony with ourselves and our inner strength enables us to also tap into this unseen power.

Intuition is an ability that can not be forced. It does not work well when you are under a great deal of stress or fretting about a situation. Intuition comes from the peace and harmony of a quiet mind—a mind that knows that the events and answers that are arriving are coming as a result of the requests that you have made in your thoughts, and that you will soon understand where, in the current situation, your answer lies. As long as you are at peace with your situation, your intuition will be able to help you with any situation.

Writing

I began writing as a self-preservation mechanism. The affirmations and mantras that I was using required complete concentration and a meditative state of awareness; that is, very relaxed and focused so that there were no distractions to inhibit the message getting firmly into my subconscious mind. When I moved myself to a comfortable and quiet location in the house and did my affirmations the repetition would put me to sleep. This frustrated me as I was not certain that I continued to do the required affirmations in my sleep, and I was concerned that I was losing the effect of reinforcing the thoughts. My favourite place for answers and ideas at that time gave me the answer I was looking for. I read my horoscope in the paper and it specifically stated that in order to make it happen I had to write it down. So I committed myself to try it, and in order to keep myself awake, I took a notebook and a pen to my meditative spot and wrote the affirmations as I repeated them. This enabled me to stay awake and to complete my sessions every day.

Soon after this answer was presented to me, I happened across Henriette Klausers' book 'Write It Down, Make It Happen.' I could not attribute this to mere coincidence so I immediately bought and devoured the book. Although I did not understand her explanation of the reticular activating system and how writing activates this filter and tells the brain that this is important, I accepted it as a necessary part of my daily routine. I have since come to realize the incredible power that writing adds to the affirmations and mantras. When you run through your affirmation in your mind when you are standing in a line up waiting for your turn, you are utilizing just the thought process. When you are in a secluded spot and you speak your affirmations out loud, not only are you processing the thought, you are also hearing it. This is like setting up an echo that reinforces the thought by introducing it through the auditory system as well. Your brain must also process the input from your ears so in essence you are getting double the repetition. When you think your affirmation, and speak it aloud as you write it down, you have engaged three different agencies to pass the message along; Thought, Hearing, and Seeing (reading). You have thus engaged your RAS filter to indicate that this is important stuff and should be processed as such, in addition to your processing of the auditory input and the original thought patterns.

Writing also expands the flexibility of your exploration of what you are asking for. Putting pen to paper has a way of waking up the creative side of your brain so that you can drift into new ideas and concepts and perhaps advance the idea or the plan that you have embarked upon. You may find that what you thought you were asking for is no longer specifically what you want, and that you need to modify your requests to meet your new goals. Writing also helps to slow down the brain and keep it focused on the concepts that you are reinforcing. A person thinks at around 500 words per minute, speaks at approximately 200 words per minute, but can write at only 20 words per minute. As you train your mind to focus on the words you are writing and keep it from wandering, you will further strengthen the message by its purity.

I found that writing allowed me to further calm my mind, and, as I allowed myself to become absorbed in the writing, the answers to questions that I was searching for would come to me even before I was finished writing. I had results from all of the techniques that I have discussed, but when I began writing, everything went to a whole new level. My writing expanded from my affirmations, to exploring ideas and new plans, to giving thanks for the answers that could not wait until I was finished asking. There is undeniable truth in writing it down to make it happen.

Tithe

Among the novel ideas to be found in this book, tithe is perhaps one of the most controversial. The understanding of tithe as derived from the biblical account is that the tenth part of your issue is sacred unto the Lord. For those who follow the letter of the law according to Leviticus, the giving to others in need is in addition to this. Whatever your personal beliefs on this issue, there is no doubt that when we give, we also receive. "Give, and it shall be given unto you; good measure, pressed down, and shaken together, and running over, shall men give into your bosom. For with the same measure that ye mete withal it shall be measured to you again." Luke 6, 38.

This is explained in different ways by different authors, and all of them make sense to me. The giving of those things you do not really need to those who do need them reduces the clutter in your life and helps to establish the harmony that will attract the new items that will replace the old that you have given away. Giving of that which you need and use establishes a gap in the energy of your harmonious existence and the universe will work to refill that gap. Giving in love and with compassion helps to establish the energy that is required in order for you to receive. One of the books I read stresses that we not ever refuse a gift even if we know that the person giving it can not really afford to give it. In so doing we can block the energy that the giver is creating that will allow them to receive back the blessings generated by their gift.

To give whether as a tithe, or to a charity or a charitable organization, should never be given grudgingly or in expectation of a return, but freely and willingly, knowing that the blessings are in the giving. Neither is giving simply a matter of money or material goods. The most precious thing that we have to give is our time, even if it is just the time it takes to say thank you to a stranger for some small deed.

I have struggled for years over the concept of tithing and giving, and have decided that the emphasis should be on giving and the mental state that establishes the energy and thought patterns that are conducive to our existence in harmony. One of my affirmations that I adapted from Joseph Murphy states that "Money flows through me freely, copiously, endlessly and I am forever being reminded of my true worth." I have adopted the same attitude with those things that I can give other than money, possessions, time, knowledge, and support. As I give I know I will receive for that is the law of the universe. How you give will be determined by your heart and your beliefs.

Put Your Mind Where Your Heart Is

There is a huge difference between stoically accepting whatever life brings you and honestly believing that what you are receiving is part if the Infinite plan for your life. When you adopt the views that I have presented in this book you are taking control of your life by attracting from the universe those things which you want for yourself. You do this by changing your patterns of thought to those of peace, harmony and love; and these you attract to yourself along with success and wealth. This new mind set enables you to know, without a doubt, that in whatever comes your way there is the answer that you are asking for, or that the answer is almost there and this little detour is somehow part of the plan.

Do not confuse this with the similar, but self defeating mind-set of the martyr. The martyr sees the failure of their aspirations to manifest themselves and consciously decides to suffer in silence. They think there is some benefit to them in accepting any ill that comes their way, passively, as their lot in life. This infers to the subconscious mind that they somehow deserved to not receive the riches they requested; that they for some reason were being rewarded with hardship. The riches in wealth, riches in health, riches in family, etc. have for some reason been denied them for a greater good. If you allow your mind to pull you into that trap then you are attracting those disappointments and they will come. You cannot change the laws of the universe. The law of gravity requires that you leave the legs on your table no matter how much you want them out of the way of your knees. You can only learn to utilize them for your good or ill. Job, in the old testament of the bible has been for centuries the stalwart example of the martyr. However, even before his trials began he had invited disharmony into his family. He offered burnt offerings for all of his sons every day; "for Job said, It may be that my sons have sinned, and cursed God in their hearts", Job 1, 5. When afflicted with boils as the second test and he cursed the day he was born he also said "For the thing which I greatly feared is come upon me, and that which I was afraid of is come unto me." Job 3, 25. Did not Job by his very thoughts and actions offer an access route for misfortune?

When we look at the peace and harmony of the universe, and the laws that hold this loose collection of atoms together in a miracle of form and function, can we doubt that harmony is not supposed to be our natural state? If that is the case, then it must be that if we are not in harmony that we are somehow not operating within the framework of the design of the universe and its laws. Do we not have every right to expect that the Infinite power that holds our universe together wants for us nothing but the same harmony and success? "And I say unto you, Ask, and it shall be given you; seek, and ye shall find; knock, and it shall be opened unto you. For every one that asketh receiveth; and he that seeketh findeth; and to him that knocketh it shall be opened. If a son shall ask bread of any of you that is a father, will he give him a stone? Or if *he ask* a fish, will he for a fish give him a serpent? Or if he shall ask an egg, will he offer him a scorpion?" Luke 11, 9-12.

Whatever your ideas on religion, or whatever Deity you acknowledge, there is a belief that such a power exists. Whether you base your existence solely on the biblical account or whether you tend to lean more toward one of the other great leaders and teachers, you do believe in a Deity that possesses great power and all knowledge. All of humanities religions are secure in the knowledge that their Deity is all powerful and can answer their prayers should He so desire and find you worthy. It is this faith in the ultimate power and capability of our God that enables us to believe that He will answer our prayers and requests; that He will give us the answers we seek in any way that He sees fit, and that He wants for us nothing but the best. To think anything else is to diminish the omnipotence of our Deity and to place our concepts above His.

I have credited each of the authors that have gone before me with the concepts, explanations and ideas that I was led to in their writings, because I believe in giving credit where credit is due. While I realize that the concepts did not originate with these authors, I am grateful that they had the unselfish desire to share their insights, in an attempt to offer others a chance at a better life. That I was led to their explanations and that each conveyed to me, through their writings, the energy that I needed to take myself to the next level, is a tribute to their intuition and generosity. I have seen first hand the confirmation that the knowledge they wanted to pass on works. I, in turn, pass on to you that achievement is available to anyone who will embrace these concepts, commit themselves to change their destiny, and persevere until they succeed.

Lectures

"Put Your Mind Where Your Heart Is" was written to compliment Noelle's series of personal power development and disease prevention lectures. Her weekend seminar series illustrates, teaches and expands on the techniques mentioned in this book. This inspirational and motivational seminar will make the path to your dreams one that you can walk as you learn how to overcome obstacles of self-doubt, financial trouble, and fear.

For information about scheduled weekend seminars and lectures, or to book Noelle for a speaking engagement, please visit www.noellejellison.com.

Acknowledgements

I wish to express my appreciation to the authors of all the books that I was led to, and whose insights inspired and motivated me to pursue the knowledge that I needed to achieve my dreams.

James Allen
Claude M. Bristol
Dr. Wayne Dyer
Shakti Gawain
Napoleon Hill
John Kehoe
Ken Keyes Jr.
Henriette Anne Klauser
Dr. Joseph Murphy
Suze Orman
Florence Shovel Shinn

ISBN 1412080649